A Better Ending

and Other Short Stories for Boys and Girls

DOREEN TAMMINGA

Reformation Heritage Books
Grand Rapids, Michigan

A Better Ending
© 2020 by Doreen Tamminga

Reformation Heritage Books
2965 Leonard St. NE
Grand Rapids, MI 49525
616–977–0889
orders@heritagebooks.org
www.heritagebooks.org

Printed in the United States of America
20 21 22 23 24 25/10 9 8 7 6 5 4 3 2 1

Interior illustrations by Doreen Tamminga
Cover art by Corine Postma

Library of Congress Cataloging-in-Publication Data

Names: Tamminga, Doreen. author.
Title: A better ending : and other short stories for boys and girls / Doreen Tamminga.
Description: Grand Rapids, Michigan : Reformation Heritage Books, [2020] | Includes index. | Audience: Ages 9-12. | Summary: "A collection of short stories and poems that encourage young readers to reflect on their own hearts and lives as they relate to God's Word"—Provided by publisher.
Identifiers: LCCN 2020021190 (print) | LCCN 2020021191 (ebook) | ISBN 9781601787903 (paperback) | ISBN 9781601787910 (epub)
Subjects: LCSH: Christian life—Literary collections. | CYAC: Christian life—Literary collections.
Classification: LCC PZ7.T16116 Be 2020 (print) | LCC PZ7.T16116 (ebook) | DDC [Fic]—dc23
LC record available at https://lccn.loc.gov/2020021190
LC ebook record available at https://lccn.loc.gov/2020021191

*For additional Reformed literature, request a free book list from
Reformation Heritage Books at the above regular or email address.*

For my mom,

who has never stopped appreciating a well-told story.
May this book be a blessing, joining the ranks of those
that speak truth in a winsome way.

Contents

From the Author ix

1. A Better Ending 1
   "Small Steps" 7

2. A Higher Purpose 8
   "Instruments of Praise" 13

3. Hand-Me-Down Dog 14
   "Day by Day" 19

4. The Red Geranium 20
   "Let Them Come to Me" 26

5. When the Rains Came 27
   "Just a Little Cloud" 33

6. Caiman and Camelids 34
   "White as Snow" 42

7. The Ruins 43
   "Heroes of the Faith" 49

8. Second Chances 50
   "Blessings from Above" 57

9. French for Rachel 58
   "Planned with Care" 63

10. The Swindler 64
    "Tangled in Sin" 70

11. Patches's Way 71
    "The Saddest Sight to See" 77

12. Sweeter than Them All 78
    "Today Is the Day" 84

13. Too Much Chatter 85
    "Creatures of the Deep" 92

14. Surprised by Joy 93
    "Meantime" 100

15. Behind the Backstop 101
    "Closer than a Brother" 107

16. Wait for Me! 108
    "To Serve His Way" 112

17. Missing! 113
    "Jesus, Shepherd" 120

18. Ahead of the Storm 121
    "My Feathered Friend" 128

19. A Break from Spring Break 129
    "The Master's Way" 136

20. Laughter in the Woods 137
    "Who Am I?" 143

21. Someone Special 144
    "The House of God" 149

22. Treasures and Daydreams 150
    "What God Has Given Me" 156

23. Better than Sacrifice 157
    "Be Holy" 162

24. Camping Woes and Wonders 163
    "Two Words" 168

25. Hungry Inside 169
    "Tell Me" 174

Topical Index 175

From the Author

In your hands you hold a book of stories—stories that will take you from your home and school, across the world, and back to your own backyard again! You'll be meeting kids with hopes and worries just like yours—kids who are learning what a life lived for the glory of God looks like. It is my prayer that these stories will also serve as a mirror—that as these characters see their need for grace, you will see a reflection of your own thirsty soul and the God who gives grace freely to anyone who asks.

You are growing older now, and every day you are making choices about what will fill your mind and eyes, ears and hands. I hope that you will choose carefully, keeping in mind the apostle Paul's instruction to think about whatever is true, honest, pure, lovely, and worthy of praise. If you are looking for encouragement about a certain topic, turn to the topical index in the back of this book. It will help you find stories on friendship and faith, teasing and tempers, patience and prayer, and so much more!

May God bless these stories to your heart and life. For more stories, poems, songs, or coloring pages, ask your parents to help you print some off at aneverydayfaith.com.

—*Doreen*

1. A Better Ending

"Oh, Mom! Can we get one? Please!" Caleb and his two younger sisters crowded around Mom as she typed out the program for the Sunday school program. "They're the cutest kittens, and they're *free!*"

Mom sighed and pushed back her chair. "Honey," she said, "you know I'm allergic to cats. I'm sorry, but you know we can't get one." And she turned back to the computer.

"No cat—no dog," Caleb grumbled as he turned away.

"That's 'cause Mom's allergic to cats and Dad says dogs belong on a farm—not in the city," Miriam piped up.

"I know, I know," Caleb said irritably. He had known the answer would be no, but still, somehow, he had hoped.

"Oh well," Naomi said sensibly. "There's nothing we can do about it. Let's set up your doll-house, Miriam."

But Miriam wasn't finished. "How come Mom didn't change her mind?" she asked Naomi as they headed upstairs. "You said to pray about it, and maybe God would hear our prayer."

Caleb didn't hear Naomi's answer as the two girls disappeared into their bedroom to

play make-believe with their dolls. Lonely, he dropped down on the couch and sighed. *How could you make-believe a cat? A cat would be so cool in the house.*

Caleb loved wild animals and would come home from school each week with several new library books on Africa and the animals of its plains or jungles. Name any animal, and he could tell you its family, habitat, eating habits—everything! And cats—well, they were the closest he would ever come to owning a lion or lynx or bobcat, Caleb was sure.

Rrr-iow! Caleb had finished his homework and gone out to bring the recycling bin to the road. *Rrr-iow!* In a bid for attention, the cat wound its orange body around his leg. Caleb's eyes brightened. *Now this was an awesome tiger-looking cat.* As he bent to stroke its striped fur, it crouched for the leap to the fence top. There it stared at him, at last winking one eye. Caleb winked back and swallowed down his longing. "Go home, Cat," he said. "You already have a master."

That was what was so cool about cats, he thought as the cat ran effortlessly along the fence. *Cats could prowl the neighborhood as though they owned it, slipping in and out of yards unseen. No fence would keep them out. But still, when the night became too cold and their stomachs were empty and their backs were longing for a human touch, like a needle drawn north in its compass, cats would set their course for home and comfort—each one seeking out a lap to curl up on.*

When Caleb stepped out the front door for school the next morning, he glanced at the porch and was surprised to see the light dusting of snow crisscrossed in cat paw prints. And coming home from school, he was even more surprised when the cat leaped down the porch steps to greet him. Scooping it up in his arms, Caleb burst into the house. "Look, Mom! It must be hungry! It's so skinny and probably has no home! Can we keep it?"

Mom sighed. "You may feed it," she said at last.

The children fed the cat. For two days it disappeared during the daytime but always came back for a meal and a place to sleep. When Mom said little as she rubbed her itchy eyes and reached for the tissue box, the children's hopes began to rise.

On the third night, Dad had just finished the Bible reading after supper when Miriam spoke up. "Dad," she asked, "does God always answer prayer?"

Dad placed the bookmark in the Bible and set it on the shelf. "Yes," he said at last. "God does answer all true prayers, but we need to be patient. His time is not our time." Mom sneezed. "And," Dad continued while looking at the cat, "the Lord sometimes answers in a different way than we expect."

Caleb thought about that. He wasn't sure he liked Dad's answer. He had wanted Dad to say, "Yes, God always answers prayer, immediately, just the way we want Him to." But Caleb knew that this was his sinful, selfish nature speaking.

Ding-dong! The doorbell interrupted the washing of the supper dishes. When his sisters didn't respond to the bell, Caleb ran to the door. A boy about his own age was handing out homemade "Lost!" notices.

"You did see my cat?" he asked in halting English. "My family gone and back and cat gone. Lost, maybe. No food!" His voice trembled.

Caleb's heart sank. He glanced over his shoulder to make sure the cat wasn't in view.

"Uh, that's too bad," he stuttered out and reached for a "Lost!" paper. "We'll, uh, let you know if we see it."

As the evening wore on, Caleb couldn't concentrate on his homework. He felt such guilt that at last he showed Dad the paper. The description matched that of their "borrowed" cat. "I'm, uh, almost done with my homework, so I thought I'd bring the cat over now," Caleb said.

Dad nodded and looked Caleb in the eye. "I think that's a very good idea," he said.

The address was for a home on the other side of the block, and Caleb was soon climbing the crumbling porch steps. Raising a hand, he knocked loudly against the peeling painted door. The boy's mother opened the door. She spoke even less English than her son, apparently. But as the boy also appeared in the doorway, the cat leaped from Caleb's arms onto the boy's chest, where it curled over his shoulder. *Rrr-iow!*

"Oh! You found!" the boy exclaimed. "You like cat?"

Looking away, Caleb nodded.

"You come play with cat," the boy continued.

"Yes!" his mother nodded eagerly. "Come," she said, and pointed to their home and then to her son. "Miguel friend! Yes?"

Now Caleb looked carefully at the other boy. With his poor English, he probably didn't have many friends. And then there was the cat… "Tomorrow," he promised. "I'll come tomorrow."

And Caleb did. Right after school he arrived, and Miguel was there to welcome him. Night came early at this time of the year, and it didn't seem long before Caleb had to leave. Bursting back into his own home, he could hardly stop talking. "And they have hardly any furniture in their house!" he told Mom, "and their dad is always working, and their mom cleans people's houses, and there's an old grandfather who lives there too, and Miguel's little sister…"

Caleb went on and on to his parents about the poor immigrant family who lived just on the other side of the block.

The smell of turkey in gravy, buttery mashed potatoes, and sugared carrots filled the house. *Ah-choo!* Mom sneezed, and Miguel's mother laughed. "Cat?" she asked. And Mom nodded as she grabbed another tissue. Dad was sitting at the kitchen table with Miguel's father. Because of his work, the man knew more English than his wife. Empty coffee cups rested between them, and Dad was talking earnestly about God's care and guiding in their own family life.

Miriam and Naomi had brought down their dolls and were playing house with Miguel's sister. Her eyes shone as she brushed a doll's long, silky hair. Caleb and Miguel were entertaining themselves with the cat's antics. It had been a good idea to invite Miguel and his family to join them for the Christmas program and sing-along.

Miguel's parents had accepted the invitation eagerly. It seemed that they had as few friends in this new country as their son. The old grandfather had not come with them to the church service, but the thought of a good meal had drawn him over for dinner, and he sat in a corner of the living room now, watching the children play with the cat and listening to the progress of the meal preparation.

Pounce! The cat swiped at the shoelace Caleb slithered across the floor. Here it was, a cat welcomed by Mom in his own living room. Caleb paused in his play to glance at Dad. Dad looked up and caught his gaze. He smiled at Caleb. *See?* he seemed to say as he took in the cat and the new neighbor family that had joined them. *You need patience, my boy. God does answer prayer, in His own time and in His own way.*

SMALL STEPS

Drip by drip, too slow to see,
An icicle grows as big as me!
Creeping high but moving slow,
I cannot see the pole bean grow.
I stretch as tall as tall can be—
Can't wait to see the grown-up me!

With small, small steps a mountain's climbed…
The upward hike takes so much time!
Yet since from God comes each new day,
I will not rush the hours away
But use them well and one day see
What drips and steps will come to be!

2. A Higher Purpose

"Yes, I'm sure she would be able to play for you," Mom said into the phone. "Yes…yes. We'll be there at seven. Goodbye."

Chrissy looked up as Mom set down the receiver. "Who has to play?" she asked with suspicion.

"The youth group has a meditation and hymn sing at the seniors' home tonight," Mom said. "Lynn usually plays the piano for them, but she was called in to work."

"So they asked me?" Chrissy interrupted. She felt her stomach sink as Mom nodded yes.

Chrissy was still nervous when she walked into the large room that evening. She was too young to join the church youth group yet, so she had never visited the seniors' home with them before. Chrissy didn't know what would be expected of her. *Will I have to talk to the residents?* she wondered. *What should I say if they speak to me?* And what about playing the piano? She knew many hymns, but what if someone chose one she had never heard of?

"You'll do fine," her mother had assured her. "You can always just pick out the melody if it's a difficult piece."

<hr/>

Closing the piano lid, Chrissy got up from the piano bench. *That's done,* she thought with relief, but she knew she wouldn't be able to relax until they were back in the car. Clutching the hymnal, she moved awkwardly toward the door. Mom was talking with an old gentleman confined to a wheelchair. *Hopefully she will be ready to go soon,* Chrissy thought.

One of the residents reached out to her as she passed. "I used to play the piano too, hon," the old woman said, grasping Chrissy's hand eagerly. "Oh, how I could make that instrument sing! I wasn't just a beginner, you know. I had talent—real talent, my piano teacher said. But, there, I shouldn't go bragging on myself!" And she laughed at her own joke.

Chrissy shuffled her feet uneasily as the woman went on. "You taking lessons, hon? Who's your teacher?" Chrissy opened her mouth to respond but never got the chance. "It's been lovely having you; you come again, do you hear?"

"Yes, Mrs.—" Chrissy hesitated, taking in the bright jewelry and colorful scarf.

"Aunty May, hon," the woman said and laughed again. "It's just Aunty May. Folks around here all call me that. You know, I expect I've been called Aunty May as long as I can remember!"

"Yes, Aunty May," Chrissy said, wondering how to excuse herself. "I—"

"Now, you just run along, hon," Aunty May interrupted. "I can see your mother coming for you." And the old woman shooed Chrissy away with one ring-bedecked hand.

"Do I have to play again?" Chrissy complained. "This is the fourth time this year! Besides, I have a project to work on for school."

"Your project can wait," Mom said. "These visits and singing from the youth mean a lot to the elderly. Besides, you have a talent for playing the piano. I know it takes a lot of practice, but now you can use your gift to cheer others."

Chrissy sighed and got up. She supposed Mom was right. The music probably did brighten the long days of those shut in at the seniors' home. Still, her steps slowed as they entered the large room where the seniors were gathered. If only no one would talk to her.

"Go on, now," her mother urged as they waited for the meditation to begin. "Aunty May will be waiting for you."

On Chrissy's second visit, Aunty May had taken both of her hands in her own and told her all about her hometown, about the small country church she had attended and the choir she had sung in. Last month she had seemed a little tired but started talking when she saw the flowers Mom had urged Chrissy to bring. Clutching the cluster of flowers in both hands, Aunty May described her first home and the large rose garden she had kept.

"Oh, you should have seen the garden in June, hon. I had the biggest old-fashioned roses you've ever seen: pale yellows and creams, warm pinks and peaches, and deep reds. And the fragrance! I could sit for an hour every evening, just thinking and praying. The peace often lifted my thoughts to heaven, to Emmanuel's land. It never failed to refresh my spirit."

She grew quiet then, as quickly as she had begun. Resting the flowers on her lap, she said sadly, "I can't seem to find that place anymore, hon. The roses and the refreshing—they're gone now, hon. I just can't find them." Even the hymn singing hadn't seemed to cheer her that night.

Aunty May seemed weaker still this evening. Her colorful scarf was missing, and only the rich scent of perfume greeted Chrissy as she sat down next to the old woman.

"Hi, Aunty May," Chrissy said, forcing a smile. When she received no answer, she reached for the old woman's hands. But Aunty May only rocked slightly back and forth, her fingers absentmindedly picking at a thread in her skirt.

Chrissy swallowed back the big lump that had formed in her throat. A well of compassion suddenly rose up in her heart for this lonely old woman. Suddenly she wanted to show Aunty May that she cared about her, cared enough to come and visit, to hear her stories, to gladden her with her piano playing. In her heart rose the desire to use this God-given talent to cheer other lonely hearts. Quietly she held the old woman's hand during the meditation, then got up to play for the hymn singing.

The singing was drawing to an end. Flipping through the hymnal, Chrissy searched for the hymn that Aunty May had spoken of, the one about Emmanuel's land. There it was. Mustering up her courage, Chrissy called out one more request: "'The Sands of Time Are Sinking,' please, if we have time." Firmly, she played the opening chords, and the youth began to sing:

> The sands of time are sinking,
> The dawn of heaven breaks;
> The summer morn I've sighed for—
> The fair, sweet morn awakes:
> Dark, dark had been the midnight
> But dayspring is at hand,
> And glory, glory dwelleth
> In Emmanuel's land.

Chrissy glanced at the old woman as she played. Slowly the rocking ceased, and Aunty May raised her head. Recognition crossed her face as her eyes struggled to focus on the pianist. Her lips began to move faintly, struggling to form the words, and by the second verse tears were slipping down her cheeks.

> O Christ, He is the fountain,
> The deep, sweet well of love!
> The streams on earth I've tasted,
> More deep I'll drink above.

The words of the hymn ran through Chrissy's mind on the way home. Seeing how deeply the words had touched Aunty May had opened Chrissy's eyes. She saw now that there was a higher purpose to her music. Before, she had used her God-given talent of piano playing only to cheer others with the music. Now she saw that the melodies could be a blessing for their spirits as the music brought back words hidden long ago in their hearts. And that was a great privilege, wasn't it? To point others to Jesus as their lives came to an end, to point them to their only Hope and to give comfort to His children as they drew near to Emmanuel's land.

INSTRUMENTS OF PRAISE

(Psalm 150)

I'll play the flute when I am grown,
So sweet and high and clear;
I'll play the trumpet, pure of sound,
A song for all to hear.

And if I can, I'll also play
The cymbals or the drum;
I'll draw a bow across the strings
To make the big bass hum.

I'll play the organ, loud and strong
Or sure and soft and mellow;
I'll pluck the strings to hear them ring
On violin and cello.

I think I'll play the tuba, too—
I love its oomphy sound;
I'll play the piano high and low
Till music shakes the ground!

When I am grown I'll play them all
In praises to the King,
But while I'm small, I still shall raise
My voice to God and *sing!*

3. Hand-Me-Down Dog

Thwack! The baseball slapped against Joe's glove and bounced into the grass behind him. Joe could feel his face growing red as he scrambled to retrieve the ball. Quickly he tossed it to second base. Too late—the runner was safe. "It's this awful glove," Joe grumbled to himself. "It's way too big."

When Joe had asked his parents for a baseball glove to use at school, he had hoped for a new one, not Uncle Mike's hand-me-down glove. But Dad had said there was no money for a new glove. At least Joe could now join the other boys in playing baseball at lunch hour. "But the team would have been better off without me," Joe mumbled. "This glove is too big for me to grip the baseball. I haven't made a single catch."

When the bell signaled the end of recess, Joe dragged his feet along behind the rest of the boys. He didn't want to hear the praise for Philip, their team's star player.

Dinner hour brought more bad news. Dad and Mom had promised Joe that he could get a dog for his twelfth birthday. During supper, Joe casually mentioned that his birthday was only a few weeks away. "That's right," Mom said, "so we should see about a visit to the animal shelter. Maybe we can go this Saturday."

The animal shelter? Joe's fork clattered down on his plate in surprise. *What kind of funny-looking dog would they find there?* He had envisioned a beautiful chocolate lab puppy. A dog he could be proud to show off at Uncle Mike's soccer games…a dog as impressive as Philip's.

⋅⋅⋅

Joe helped Mom lift the crate into the back seat of the van. "I suppose he's alright," he said in answer to Mom's question. But his thoughts were quite different: *first a hand-me-down glove and now a hand-me-down dog.*

The dog poked his head out of the crate, and Joe looked at him once again. A mixed mutt, he was kind of cute with one ear perked up and one half flopped over—but not the bundle of chocolate fur that Joe had hoped for.

⋅⋅⋅

The next few days were busy as Joe and the puppy grew used to each other. It was a lot of work taking care of a puppy, even one that was nearly grown. Joe was becoming discouraged with Cleo.

"Be patient," Mom told Joe. "He'll soon be a dog you can be proud of."

But that was just the problem.

After supper, Joe pulled out his bike to head over to the soccer field.

Dad spotted him as he was coming out of the garage. "Why don't you take Cleo along?" he asked.

"Nah, I'd rather not," Joe said. He avoided Dad's eyes. "He might get into trouble."

"You're not embarrassed by him, are you?" Dad asked.

At first Joe shrugged, but then the whole story spilled out—how Philip was always tops in everything. Philip was the best baseball player, the most popular boy in the class, and he even had the nicest dog. He took him to all the soccer games, and everyone petted him and praised his beautiful golden fur. The dog would sit there like a statue, regal and tall, living up to his name, King.

"You know something, Joe?" Dad said as he closed the garage door. "You're looking for happiness in all the wrong places. Being popular and being the best will make you feel good for only a little while. It won't make you truly happy. Trying to live life your own way never does."

Joe frowned in concentration. *What does Dad mean?* he wondered.

Dad explained. "Serving God is the only thing that brings lasting happiness. Instead of planning ways to get the most attention from your friends, you need to start studying God's plan for your life. You will find out that His way is to have you serve *others*, to bring *them* happiness. Do you see what I mean?"

"A little," Joe said. *Somehow Dad was saying that not trying to do things for yourself would make you happier than trying to please yourself. But how could that be?* Joe hopped on his bike and waved goodbye. He would have to think about this some more. And in the meantime, Cleo would stay home.

"Heel," Joe commanded, and stopped in the middle of the sidewalk. It must have been the fifth or sixth day of taking walks, but Cleo still bounced happily from the grass on one side of the sidewalk to the road on the other.

"Heel!" Joe ordered again loudly. Cleo paused, cocked his head at Joe as though to say, "Come on! What are you waiting for?" and darted eagerly ahead. *Snap!* The leash went taut, and Joe was jerked along behind.

Reeling in the dog like a fish on a line, Joe pulled Cleo to his side. "You are walking right beside me, whether you want to or not!" Joe said through gritted teeth. But Cleo refused to settle into Joe's pace. Straining against his collar, he gasped his way along.

"You know something, Cleo?" Joe asked the panting dog as they struggled down the sidewalk. "You're looking for happiness in all the wrong places. You think that pleasing yourself will make you happy. You want to run across a busy road. But if you would just stick to the limit of the leash, you would have plenty of freedom."

Joe stopped abruptly as he heard his own words. *Was that the answer? If Cleo would be happier by accepting the limits Joe put on him with the leash…wouldn't that be true for Joe too? Hadn't God set limits and laws for people's own good?* Joe started walking again, but he didn't stop thinking. *That must have been what Dad meant when he said I have to start studying God's plans instead of my own. His plan for happiness is much different from mine.*

"Come on, boy!" he called as he broke into a run. "I'll race you home!"

◆◆▷———◁◆▷———◁◆

That night Joe took Cleo along to the soccer game. Cleo managed to wrap himself around the light pole, worm his way under a man's chair to get a half-eaten burger, and trip Joe half a dozen times with the leash.

Joe scolded the dog as he happily wagged his tail and then scowled at Philip's dog. There King sat, the model of perfect behavior. "Down, boy!" Joe scolded as Cleo jumped up with both paws to snuffle his shirtfront. King never moved. *He's like a statue…,* Joe suddenly thought, *rather lifeless.*

Cleo paid King no attention. Pulling Joe along, he was busy entertaining the babies in their strollers. They each got a free face wash. His snuffling nose found any leftover bits of supper tucked in baby necks or stuck between sticky fingers. When at last Joe dragged him over to a nearby bench, Cleo dropped right on Joe's feet. His eyes never left Joe's face. "It's okay," the dog seemed to say. "I know you want me right beside you. And that's okay. I'm starting to like it—just as long as we're together."

Thwack! The baseball slapped against Joe's glove and bounced out behind him. No problem. Cleo was right there to catch it.

"Here, boy!" Joe called.

The dog bounced triumphantly across the lawn, his shaggy tail waving like a proud flag. After a few keep-aways, he dropped the ball at Joe's feet.

"Good boy," Joe praised. "You're starting to learn!" He tossed the ball back to Dad.

"And so are you," Dad added.

DAY BY DAY

When I hear God's Word
And I think on it—
On His love and tender grace
To one like me
Who would follow Him
But forgets to seek His face—

Then I pause, amazed
At how kind God is—
That He still invites my prayers—
And my heart grows warm
With new love for Him
As I see how much He cares.

Yet I turn away
And refuse to play
With a friend who wants *my* love.

And I shirk my work,
Roll my eyes at Mom,
Give my brother a little shove.

Then the skies of my heart
Grow gray and cold
As the winds of sin blow strong,
Till I hear His voice
Calling me to turn
From the path of sin I am on.

Like a deer I fly
From the tempter's bow
That would pierce me through with sin.
Panting after God,
I repent of sin
And am washed by His blood again.

4. The Red Geranium

The road had disappeared. Only two packed-down tire tracks marked the way, but they were lost every few seconds in the great gusts of snow that swept across their path. Mom's hands clutched the steering wheel tightly as she followed the red taillights ahead of her. Kari wondered what would happen if the car ahead of them couldn't see where it was going. Would they follow it into a ditch, or a lamppost, or a tree? She had seen many snowstorms before, but usually from the safety of the house. Now her ten-year-old heart pumped with fear.

"This must be the side road here," Mom said. And crawling along at a snail's pace, she carefully eased the van around the corner.

Kari sat forward in her seat and peered through the windshield, past the swishing wipers. It was up to her to identify Mr. Ramon's house.

❖———————— ❖❖ ————————❖

Kari could clearly remember her first real meeting with old Mr. Ramon. It wouldn't be easy to forget the eggs all over the sidewalk and the gravel ground into her knees. It had happened about a month ago. Mom had sent Kari to the grocery store for a carton of eggs. Since the weather had been quite mild for January, and the snow had all melted, Kari had decided to bike. It would be quicker.

Finding the eggs had been easy, since Mom always took all the kids grocery shopping each week. But at the checkout Kari realized she had forgotten to bring a bag. Mom had given her a handful of exact change for the eggs. Kari counted it once, then twice. There wasn't even five cents extra to buy a plastic bag. She frowned, then shrugged. There was nothing she could do about it.

Climbing onto her bike, she set out slowly, resting the eggs on the handlebar with one hand and steering with the other. Things went smoothly, even turning the corner onto the side street to cut through the back roads toward home. It was when her hand started aching from clutching the large carton so tightly that things went wrong.

There was a long, straight stretch of sidewalk ahead of her, and Kari pedaled hard for a moment before stilling her legs and resting the eggs on her knees. The carton lay even as she flexed her cramped hand.

Then it happened. A small brown dog came tearing down a short driveway, yipping furiously. Kari was not generally afraid of dogs, but as the small creature jumped at her legs she pressed the pedals to hurry away. Before she knew what had happened, the eggs had slipped down, bounced off the center bar of her bike, and were sent sailing by an errant pedal. Kari's arm shot down to attempt to rescue the eggs, the steering wheel whipped sideways, and the whole lot of them careened over the curb into the street. The little dog yelped and darted away.

Kari picked herself up more slowly, crying out at the pain that shot through her knee and trying to wipe gooey egg from her jacket.

Unwanted tears spilled from her eyes as she tried to get up and lift the bike. Her knee hurt so badly, broken eggs were everywhere, and the bike wouldn't roll smoothly. Kari bent down to pick up an egg from the grass, but the tears blinded her eyes. How would she get her bike home? And any unbroken eggs? Fumbling for the egg, she stuffed it into her pocket and tried again to push the bike. It hardly moved. The front wheel was rubbing against the bike frame.

Dropping the bike to the ground, Kari also dropped down and sniffed back tears. She sat and swallowed and wiped her eyes and sniffed and wiped again. She didn't know what to do. There she sat on someone's front lawn staring across the road at a small brick house surrounded by a low fence and a garden full of dead things. Her dull eyes focused on the one bright spot: a red geranium sitting in the front window. A spot of cheer, Mom would say.

Cheer? Kari frowned. *Isn't that what Mom had said last week when she had bought the geranium for that old man? Maybe…* Kari stood up slowly and dragged her bicycle across the street. *Just maybe…* She laid down the bike on the driveway and walked up to the door of the little brick house. Before her fear could stop her, she rang the bell.

And that is how she had met Mr. Ramon from the grocery store. He had helped her inside, brought her some Band-Aids, shuffled over to the phone, and called her mom.

All because of Mom's love for others. All because of the red geranium.

⸻

Mom knew Mr. Ramon from the grocery store. He was there every Friday. Kari remembered with shame how she had avoided the old man and his long stories. How she had wandered off to look at the good things they couldn't buy. How she wished Mom wouldn't ask quite so many questions about his health or encourage the stories about when he was young. Often, when Kari returned, he would still be standing by their shopping cart, telling Mom again about the flu he'd had last month, the medications he was on, and how his new young doctor didn't know a thing. Finally, with a last pinch of the baby's cheeks and a rub for her brothers' heads, he would shuffle off.

It had been a week before Christmas when Mom had bought Mr. Ramon the geranium. Money was tight, with food prices rising and the old van slowly breaking down, but it didn't stop Mom that morning. She spied the geranium on her way to the checkout.

How Mom loved all living things. They had lots of houseplants at home, cuttings from Grandma's plants. Mom had a way of keeping them all looking as fresh and healthy as her children. But besides the bouquets of wildflowers the children picked in summer, flowers in the house were rare. And there she was, buying the old man a red geranium.

Kari read the price tag: $5.99.

"It will bring him cheer," Mom explained. "Sometimes cheer costs you only a conversation, and sometimes it costs $5.99."

"But we would like to have a red flower at our house too," Kari's brother pointed out.

Mom winked at him as she paid the cashier. "We have plenty of cheer already in our home," she said.

Kari agreed somewhat reluctantly. She didn't know she'd be so happy to see those bright flowers just a few weeks later.

The winter storm had lasted three days already, and Mom had missed Mr. Ramon at the grocery store that morning. It was evening now, and she and Kari had a hot pan of soup and some groceries for the kind man.

As the van turned into the narrow side road, there was a moment's relief from the storm. A long row of houses broke the force of the wind, and grand old trees held hands above the road, offering some protection to the travelers below. The road was swept clean in some areas and drifted over in others. Kari watched in admiration as Mom sped up to plough through a low drift that crossed the road. She worried that she wouldn't recognize the small brick house in the blinding snow, but there it was! The red geranium blazed like a beacon in the front window.

They found Mr. Ramon sitting at the kitchen table. The house was as tidy as on Kari's first visit, but the man himself was changed. Gone was the careful attention to Kari and the gentle helpfulness. The storm had made him anxious, and his nervous movements showed the strain of being trapped alone inside the house for days.

Within minutes Mom had a hot bowl of soup before him and the kettle boiling for some tea. Kari unpacked the groceries as she listened to Mom talk to Mr. Ramon about the winters of long ago: the years when snowstorms had brought sledding and a deep freeze had brought pond hockey. Kari's hands stilled as she stacked the last few items in the cupboard. At last she heard the old man—really heard him—and this time it was the voice of a young boy now trapped in a frail body. It was hard to imagine, but she thought of how she too would one day grow old and feeble.

As they said their goodbyes, Mom promised to send Dad over the next day to help shovel him out. She gestured toward the snow-covered garden outside. "There shouldn't be much more snow after this," she encouraged him with a smile. "Before you know it, you'll be planting geraniums outside."

Kari waved. She was sure she'd see the old man often that spring. This time when she met him in the grocery store or over his garden fence, she wouldn't hurry off. No, she would be glad to stay and hear the stories from a heart that was still her own age.

LET THEM COME TO ME

(Mark 10:13–16)

He pressed against his mother's cloak,
Frightened by the men
Whose angry voices pushed at them,
He hid his face again.

"He has no time for little ones.
Move on, move on," they said.
The small boy clutched his mother's hand
And ducked his curly head.

So many people thronged the Lord:
The sick, the blind, the lame.
Why would He bless a little boy?
How could He know his name?

But then the Lord's strong voice called out
For young and old to hear:
"Don't stop the little children
But let them come to Me!"

5. When the Rains Came

"There, little *podi*, little goats," Baruti said. "With all these thorn bushes surrounding the field, you will never be able to get into the crops." But the goats nudged their heads hard against Baruti's side. They did not seem pleased with the new fencing.

Baruti grabbed the ropes that dangled from their necks and headed back to the hut. "That field is soon going to be full of maize, you know," he continued. He couldn't keep from grinning as the thought of a juicy watermelon and pumpkin harvest also filled his mind. "Dad has the seeds all ready, and the rainy season is almost here," he told the goats.

Tying the goats to a stake outside the thin walls, he could hear Dad talking to Grandmother inside.

"But we *must* have the rain or we will all starve by next season," Dad was saying angrily. "And according to Tswana custom, the rain gods demand a—"

"We don't follow Tswana custom anymore," Grandmother said forcefully. "We follow Christian custom, and we will continue to *pray.*"

Dad was silent as Baruti entered the doorway.

<hr/>

And they came—gentle misty rains that softened the earth for Dad's ploughing. Mom went singing about her work, and Dad's shoulders lost their constant sag. A haze of green shot up, covering the ground and scattered trees. The day they cleared the old well and deepened it from its pool of muddy water felt like a holiday.

Baruti's heart was light, in contrast to the brooding clouds that had sent the early rains. He lay awake at night listening to the scuttle of insects as they rustled through the fresh vegetation. Breakfast was a feast, with a full bowl of goats' milk poured generously over the porridge.

But soon the creases appeared once again on Mom's and Dad's foreheads. For nothing was coming of the promised rainy season. All the misty drizzle had been just a tease, as the sun came out once again and burned down mercilessly for one day…three days, a week, then two. The green vegetation quickly shriveled. Bony ribs so recently covered by a thin layer of fat began to show again. The goats' milk dried up, and the porridge was plain again. Dad said nothing of the Tswana custom, but he would not pray. He sat for hours in the shade of the hut, tense and waiting, watching the barren skies. It was Grandmother who led the family prayers.

"God will send the rain when we need it," she said serenely. Only she and little sister remained untroubled.

"It has been four years, Mother," Mom replied flatly. "Four years without the needed rain."

The old grandmother looked off into the distance as she recited Proverbs 27:27 from memory: "'And thou shalt have goats' milk enough for thy food, for the food of thy household.' God has promised."

<hr />

"Can't you even stir the porridge without burning it?" Mom snapped at little sister in frustration. Tempers were short that morning, as Mom discovered the goats had broken free in the night and wandered off in search of food. They were the last of the family's herd. All the rest of the cattle had been sold off during the drought, a few each year, to buy food.

"If you loved those goats as much as you say you do, you'd have tied them up better," Mom had scolded Baruti angrily.

And now little sister had burned the porridge. Hastily scraping his bowl clean, Baruti hurried off after Grandmother's prayer. The remaining two animals were the family's only hope of milk if the rains did come, and their only possessions to sell for food if the rains did not come. But beyond this, since he had no playmates besides little sister, the goats had become Baruti's closest friends.

How far away can they be? Baruti worried to himself. *The goats were thin and weak; still, spurred on by hunger, they could have gone far.*

The land became more barren as he left the gentle swell of their farmland for the flat wasteland beyond. Coming to the dried-up riverbed, Baruti followed its path. *Where there was water, there would be vegetation, and animals could pick up the scent of water much better than humans. Perhaps the goats had followed this path.*

The riverbed twisted and turned, slowly but surely leading him into the Kalahari Desert. The ground grew red and sandy, and in the distance great dunes arose, shimmering in the heat. Here and there tall, brittle grass and clusters of acacia trees or giant Baobabs dotted the valleys between. When the rain came, this same desert land would be cloaked in green, and wildlife would abound. But for now Baruti had to watch for the deadly scorpions, puff adders, and cape cobras that liked to lie under the shepherd trees. Lizards and the larger springbok and wildebeest posed no threat.

Baruti went on tirelessly at first, but as the hours passed the day grew hotter, and the little water he had brought along was finished. At last, in the blistering heat of the day, he scrambled up from the riverbed to find some relief in the spotted shade of a camelthorn tree and its surrounding thicket. This was what the bushmen had been doing for centuries in the noonday heat: finding a shade tree, sitting under it, and waiting for the sun to slip below the dunes. Ducking beneath an enormous weaver's nest, Baruti was startled to hear the bleating of a goat and the answer of another.

"My little *podi*!" the boy exclaimed in delight. The heat was forgotten, and the thorns went unheeded as he pushed his way into the thicket. There they were! One poor creature was struggling against the rope caught in a thorn bush, while the other watched helplessly by. "I am coming, my little ones!" Baruti called again—but suddenly stopped, frozen in his tracks.

I must back off! was his frantic thought, but it was too late. With a movement too quick for the eye, the yellow-brown snake struck, biting the boy in the ankle. Baruti yelped in pain, even while a prayer of thanks rose from his heart that this was a large mole snake—a constrictor—and not a venomous cobra. Stumbling forward, he pushed through the remaining bushes and began untangling the goat's rope. Leading them to the shade of a shepherd tree, Baruti checked the ground for scorpions before retying the goats and dropping down to rest. His ankle ached.

The sun was dropping low in the sky when he awoke. Scrambling to his feet, Baruti quickly loosed the goats and led them back by way of the riverbed. The sand still gave off tremendous heat, and his thirst was almost more than he could bear. If only he could find a gemsbok bean, even the few bitter sips of water would give some relief. But no such plant rose in sight, and the only hope of water lay at home. Light-headed and wobbly legged, the boy pressed on.

Clouds were moving in as Baruti left the riverbed for home. A strong wind had risen, chasing the storm clouds across the sky, but Baruti had no eyes for the breathtaking sunset. He was only glad to escape the fine red sand being whipped through the air. The goats were on familiar

territory now, and Baruti dropped their ropes, letting them go. As thirsty as they were, they would head straight home.

Hurry, hurry, he told his leaden feet. *Just a little farther, and you will have water and rest too.* But his exhausted body would not obey his mind. *Just a little farther,* was Baruti's last thought before he slumped to the ground.

And now he dreamed that he was lying in the hut listening to great drops of rain smacking against the dry earth. The drops grew bigger and bigger, forming giant puddles of rain that splashed down upon the earth and flooded the dirt floor of the hut. Baruti could feel the water seeping through his mat into his clothes.

But suddenly Dad was there—and it *was* raining! Baruti shook the dream from his mind as Dad scooped him up into his arms.

"Good thing your sister saw those goats coming in from the riverbed," Dad said, "or we would never have found you."

The rain was now falling in great sheets, sweeping the dry earth with life-giving water. Dad tucked the boy's face against his shoulder, shielding it from the falling rain, but Baruti lifted his face free.

"God did send the rain, Dad," he said as water streamed down his cheeks. Rain streamed down Dad's face as well—or was it tears?

"Yes, Son," he said in a hoarse voice. "He did send the rain."

JUST A LITTLE CLOUD

(1 Kings 18:41–45)

Just a little cloud—
No bigger than your hand—
Rising from the sea,
Sent at God's command.

Just a little cloud
Growing now in size,
Dark with promised rain,
Covering the skies.

Just a little cloud,
Rain begins to fall—
Floods of rain so sweet,
Bringing hope to all.

Just a little cloud,
But the world can see
God the Lord controls
Earth and sky and sea.

6. Caiman and Camelids

"I need a vacation." Mom sighed as she set down the paintbrush. The basement had flooded a few weeks earlier, and all the drywall had to be ripped out. Mom had spent days sorting and cleaning and throwing out things that had been damaged by the water. Once Dad had put up the new drywall, she had worked hard painting: first an undercoat, then two more coats of paint. She looked tired.

"Just put me in an airplane and fly me away," she said to her two little girls as they watched her move the stepladder.

"Where will you fly to?" Stephanie asked. "Michigan?"

Michigan was the only place she knew in her four-year-old wisdom, since her aunt lived there.

Mom laughed. "No," she said, "I was thinking of something a little more exotic than that."

"What's exotic?" little Bethany wanted to know.

Mom loaded up the roller with paint as she answered. "It's something different," she explained. "Michigan is quite similar to where we live. An exotic place would be very different from here. You would feel like you were far away on a vacation."

The two girls looked at each other, unsure. "Exotic" meant that Mom wanted to go somewhere different. Pulling on their shoes, they went back outside to play. Watching Mom paint wasn't all that exotic, either, they thought.

Running to the sandbox, Stephanie had an idea. "Let's make Mom a vacation here in the backyard!" she said.

"How do we do that?" Bethany wanted to know.

"We can make it different," her sister explained, "like a different place for Mom to visit at coffee time!"

"Okay," Bethany agreed and began playing in the sand.

"This yard is all grass, so it has to be different," Stephanie decided. "We will make a big desert on the patio. Here," she told her sister, "use the shovel to fill up the wheelbarrow with sand, and then we can dump it on the patio."

Soon the two girls were busy going back and forth from the big sandbox to the patio with the wheelbarrow and buckets, pouring and spreading the sand across the concrete. At last Stephanie was satisfied with their work.

"That's good," she said as she looked around the yard. Her eyes rested on the swing set that stood next to the patio. "The desert needs a waterfall," she said. "Otherwise it will be too dry. Help me get the hose, Bethany."

It wasn't long before the girls had pulled the hose up the ladder and draped it down the slide. When they turned it on, water flowed down the slide, making a small stream through the desert.

Just then Ed and Justin came around the corner of the house. Ed stopped short with his hands still in his pockets. "What are you guys doing?" he asked in the way big brothers do.

Justin came closer for a better look. "Does Mom know you're doing this?" he asked.

"No," Stephanie answered. "It's a surprise for when Mom comes out for coffee! She wanted to go on a vacation, so we're making her one."

"Yeah," Bethany added. "She didn't want to go to Michigan, so we're making her a desert."

"I don't think a desert has a waterfall running through it," Ed said, smirking. "A desert is *dry*."

"Well," said Justin thoughtfully, "this could be in South America. The Atacama Desert runs right along the ocean there, in between the water and the mountains. It's the driest desert in the world, so it can't have a waterfall running into it." He paused as he eyed the swing set and the patio. "But there's a huge waterfall on the other side of the Andes Mountains, a waterfall way bigger than Niagara Falls." Before the girls knew what was happening, he had grabbed one end of the swing set. "We just need to turn this around the other way," he explained.

"And then we could make the Amazon River!" Ed jumped in, grabbing the other side of the swing set. Together the boys lifted the swingset and swung it around.

"There will have to be mountains here," Justin directed, "so the slide waterfall will go just past them. Grab the big tarp behind the shed, and we can hang it over the swing set to make the mountains."

The girls looked ready to cry. What were their brothers doing to their surprise? But when the boys had draped the tarp over the swingset, they cheered up. Didn't it make a splendid fort to hide in? But not for long.

"Hey, Steph!" Justin called. "You girls have to help too! Ed's setting up the slip'n slide to make the river; you girls have to get some fish or something to go in it."

"Okay!" The two girls ran off to the deck box to see what they could find. There wasn't much besides sand toys, but they did find two scoops shaped like fish and a big inflatable dolphin.

Ed laughed when he saw the dolphin. "This is a river," he said, "not the ocean!"

"Wait!" Justin said. "I think we might need it." And he dashed into the house. A moment later he reappeared with a big hardcover book on South America. "Let me see," he said, flipping through the pages. "Here! See? There are river dolphins in South America." He looked up triumphantly. "Blow it up, Steph!" he called. "We're going to need it."

And so it went. Mom's cactus collection came out of the house to adorn the desert. Since the only water source in the Atacama was water droplets that collected on the lichen growing on cacti, the girls were sent off to find moss. Sticking the moss onto the cacti was more of a challenge. Bethany kept pricking her fingers and cried. When Mitch, the dog, settled down in the desert, he was quickly renamed a camelid, a creature that resembled the Middle Eastern camel.

"What can we do for snow?" Justin wondered aloud. "We need snow and glaciers down in the south end of the yard."

"I can get one of our camping sheets," Ed volunteered, and soon a few old bed sheets were spread across the corner of the yard. For Mitch, it was just too much. He had to pounce on them, bark at them, and generally show the sheets just who was boss.

"Mitch! Get over here!" Ed shouted. "We can't have a camel running through the Antarctic or whatever."

"Actually," Justin said, "the camelids live in both desert and icy regions there."

Ed raised his eyebrows and shrugged at the dog. "Whatever," he said.

At last they had done all they could. If this weren't a South American vacation, the children wouldn't know what to call it. "I think that's it," Justin said, looking over the yard. "We should go get Mom."

"I will!" Stephanie said, and she dashed inside, slamming the door behind her.

The patio door opened a minute later, and Mom stepped out onto the deck. The children watched as her eyes grew wide. "Wo-o-o-w," she said slowly. They could tell she was surprised.

"Do you like it, Mom?" the girls asked. "Do you like your vacation?"

Mom laughed. "My vacation?" she asked. And then she laughed harder. "Is that what this is?"

The boys looked uncertain, and Mom stopped laughing. She stood up straight, holding an imaginary backpack and suitcase in her hands as she came down the deck. Sliding her sunglasses down from the top of her head, she put them on, took a deep breath, and said, "So, where am I?"

"South America!" the boys exclaimed. "Can't you tell?"

"Well, of course," Mom said. "There's the Amazon River flowing with our water bill right into the neighbor's backyard! Ed, quickly turn off the hose. I will imagine the rest of the river." She walked over to the blue-tarped swing set. "Why don't you give me a tour?" she asked. "I am a sightseer on vacation, after all."

"Okay!" the children clamored, and the boys began. "Over here is the Atacama Desert. The moss on the cactus is there to collect water droplets when fog rolls in from the ocean. The ocean is the neighbor's swimming pool over there."

"This is the rainforest," Stephanie explained, pointing to the garden. "That's why we put more plants by the bushes and hung vines on them."

"Mitch is the camel!" Bethany shouted eagerly.

"Well, like a camel," said Ed. "He's a camelid and can live in the dry desert or icy—"

"Mitch!" Justin interrupted suddenly. "Get out of there!" Mitch was racing down the slip'n slide river, chasing the slippery dolphin. "Help me get him off, Ed," Justin called, "before he rips a hole in it!"

Ed laughed and helped Justin chase the dog. "Maybe he thinks he's a giant river otter. Did you know they are the wolves of the Amazon, Mom? They can even kill caiman—things that look like alligators."

"Wow," Mom said and looked down. Stephanie was tugging on her hand for attention.

"Yeah, Mom," she said, "and the squirrels are the tiny monkeys that eat sap from the trees. We didn't have anything that could be the big monkeys."

"Yeah, or anything to be the savage jaguars," Justin added, "except the neighbor's cat, but Mitch scared it away."

"But we got the big rubber bugs from inside to be the huge, nasty insects they have there!" Ed pointed out cheerfully.

"Huge, nasty insects?" Mom repeated, rubbing her arms. "I'm not sure I like this vacation spot…"

Little Bethany laughed. "They're not real, Mommy," she said, picking up a gigantic rubber centipede.

Mom shuddered. "Do all those animals really live in South America?" she asked, pointing to the inflatable blue dolphin lying at the end of the river.

"Yeah!" the boys exclaimed together. "That's a river dolphin. It's the only kind of dolphin that doesn't live in saltwater oceans. It swims right through the rainforest!"

"Don't walk in the river, though, Mom," Stephanie warned her. "See our plastic fish? They're piranhas and will eat your toes and legs right off!"

"Is that so?" Mom asked in amazement as she considered the wet bedsheets in the southern end of the yard.

"The glaciers all melted," Justin explained.

"We didn't have that many ice cubes to start with, anyway," Ed added.

They had come to the end of their tour. Mom turned and looked at the tarps and water and sand, the cacti and houseplants and bedsheets lying jumbled all over the backyard. "What an incredible variety God has made on one single continent," she said. "You worked all afternoon creating this…um, this…"

"Vacation," Stephanie supplied.

"Vacation," Mom continued. "God just said the word, and all these things were created!"

"Yeah, and they actually all worked," Ed said, glancing at the melted ice cubes.

"And the animals all had the right kinds of food to eat and could live in the different climates," Justin added.

"God is so high above us," Mom said thoughtfully. "Our minds are so tiny, and our thoughts so small in comparison to His. That's why we must never question what He tells us to do in His word, the Bible. He is absolutely wise."

The children listened quietly. It was hard to imagine that the Creator was so powerful that He could simply speak and, in one instant, bring all these different things into being. They felt for a moment how small they were compared to God on high.

"Do we have to clean this all up today?" Stephanie asked. "Or can we show it to Dad after supper and clean it up tomorrow?"

"I think you can show it to Dad first," Mom said. "I'm sure he'll be impressed."

Ed looked at Mom. Sometimes he wasn't sure if she was joking or not. But he knew her next words were a joke.

"Well," she said, plopping down onto a rock in the rainforest. "This tourist is thirsty. Are there any coffee shops in South America? The Amazonian Tim Horton, or Ande's Donuts? What about Atacama's Desserts?"

Justin laughed, while Ed just rolled his eyes. Mom's jokes could be so corny. "I'll go get the coffee," he said.

WHITE AS SNOW

Red and yellow will make orange
If you mix them through and through.
Blue and yellow will make green—
We all know this is true.

There's another color rule
In the Bible you may know.
It's amazing, but it's true:
Red makes black as white as snow!

Jesus shed His precious blood
To wash sin's stain away.
His blood—so red—can bleach our hearts
A snowy white to stay.

7. The Ruins

A bell jingled above the door as they left the Christian bookstore. Both Maggie and her aunt clutched a paper bag in their hands. Climbing into Aunt Carla's car, Maggie quickly fastened her seat belt and opened her new book.

"What?" Aunt Carla exclaimed. "Reading already? Am I such bad company?"

"No," Maggie said reluctantly as she set the book down. "I was just seeing how it started."

Aunt Carla laughed. She could remember washing dishes for her mom with a book propped open on the windowsill in front of her.

"I used to be a bookworm too," she told her niece. "Now I mostly buy cards and other stuff at the bookstore."

"Like *JESUS* bracelets?" Maggie asked with interest. She waited until the car had pulled out onto the street before continuing.

"I saw a bunch of kids in the teen section. They all think they're Christians just because they're wearing those colored bracelets," she said, rolling her eyes. "You can tell they're really not. You should see their hair! And their earrings and nose rings…"

Aunt Carla kept her eyes on the road, but smiled. "Colored bracelets don't make a person a Christian," she agreed, "but neither does the 'right' kind of hair or jewelry."

"Well, at least I actually believe in Jesus," Maggie replied. "My dad says lots of people call themselves Christians but don't even know who God is. They just say they believe in Jesus and expect to go to heaven!"

"You know," Aunt Carla said as she slowed the car to make a turn, "even actually believing in Jesus isn't enough. Many people believe Jesus is the Savior and think that is enough to get them into heaven. What they don't realize is that they need Jesus to become their own personal Savior for their own personal sins."

"Oh," Maggie said. "That makes it harder to tell from the outside who are really Christians."

"Mm-hmm," Aunt Carla agreed. "But a true follower of Jesus has love for Him and will show it through fruits of joy and kindness and patience." She paused for a moment. "And they will want to keep God's law," she added. "Jesus said 'If you love Me, keep My commandments.'"

"I get it," Maggie said. She looked out the window, thinking about the teens she had just seen at the bookstore. "Sometimes I just use my imagination too much about people—that's what my mom says."

Aunt Carla smiled. "Perhaps you do! God calls us to examine our *own* heart first." She paused as she checked before switching lanes. "Do you mind if we stop for a coffee on the way?" she asked.

"I don't know," Maggie said slowly. "I think coffee tastes pretty gross."

"Oh, you!" her aunt laughed. "You know what I meant. You can get a hot chocolate or something else."

Maggie laughed. "Well, you *said* coffee," she retorted as they pulled into a parking lot.

As the car merged into traffic on the highway, Maggie curled her fingers around the warm brown cup. She took a sip of her hot chocolate and gave a contented sigh. She loved going places with Aunt Carla. She was so much fun. Maybe it was because Aunt Carla was younger than her other aunts. She was still going to school, actually! She was studying graphic design and wanted to be a photographer one day.

Maggie peered ahead out the dirty windshield as the car left the highway. "Are we almost there yet?" she asked. "I can't wait to see the ruins! Are they really from a real castle, or watchtower or whatever?"

Aunt Carla smiled. "Yes!" she said. "About ten more minutes. And the castle has been restored, although it's more like an enormous, fancy home than a castle. The watchtower is still in ruins, so you can pretend you're back in medieval times."

Maggie lifted her backpack up onto her lap and checked to make sure her pencils were sharpened. "I hope we have enough time to sketch the watchtower," she said as she zipped the pockets closed.

"Well, that depends on how long it takes you to sketch it!" her aunt replied. "Anyway, I can take a picture of it so you can finish your drawing at home."

"Here we are," Aunt Carla announced as the car entered the parking lot. "Now, do you want to visit the castle down here or hike on up to see the ruins?"

"Let's go see the ruins," Maggie suggested. "That sounds more interesting than a fancy house." She slung her backpack over her shoulder as Aunt Carla grabbed her purse from the back seat.

The cool air felt fresh after the car ride, and the bright sunshine made it feel warmer than it was. Following the steep path, the two wound their way through the woods. They were soon out of breath. "Here, let's rest for a moment," Aunt Carla suggested, stopping at a fallen log.

A soft green haze was just beginning to cover the trees overhead as new leaves began to unfold. The exercise had made her warm, and Maggie pulled off her coat. Aunt Carla bent to photograph the shoots of green that were barely poking up between the brown leaves on the forest floor.

"Okay! Let's go!" Maggie said, stuffing her coat into her backpack. Just around the bend in the trail she could see the ruins towering on the cliff above her. "It's still a long way!" she exclaimed.

"Yup," said Aunt Carla. "We still have to cross the ravine and then climb a flight of stairs."

And now Maggie saw the ravine. It wasn't very wide at all, but she paused to notice how *deep* it was. A board and rope bridge spanned its yawning gap. "We have to cross *that*?" she asked.

"Sure," her aunt replied. "It's just a couple of quick steps."

But Maggie slowed as they reached the bridge. She could see the strong cable securing the bridge on either end, but she couldn't help thinking it looked so *wobbly*!

Aunt Carla crossed quickly, running her hands lightly along the rope handrails on each side. She turned back. "Coming?" she asked. "It's strong enough; you're not as heavy as me!"

Still Maggie hesitated. It wasn't that she didn't believe her aunt. She didn't actually think the bridge would break. And with the railings on either side it wasn't actually possible to fall off, but…

"Don't you believe me?" Aunt Carla asked, crossing back to Maggie's side.

"Yeah, I do believe you. I know it's strong enough," Maggie struggled to explain. "I guess I'm just scared," she admitted, swallowing the lump in her throat. "My head knows the bridge won't break, but my feet don't believe it."

Aunt Carla threw back her head and laughed. "You sound like our catechism teacher," she said while grasping Maggie's arm. "He used that kind of analogy to explain false faith. Just like we talked about earlier, some people think that believing that Jesus is the Savior is enough. But that's all in their heads. They have never experienced salvation. Their feet have never crossed the bridge."

Maggie was listening intently. "Like me," she suddenly said in surprise as she glanced at the solid ground beneath her feet. "How did you do that?" she exclaimed before answering her own question. "You distracted me! We crossed the bridge and I didn't even realize it!"

Aunt Carla grinned. But then her face grew serious. "But you understand the difference, don't you? It's not enough for you or me to believe that Jesus is the Savior; you have to experience salvation personally."

Maggie nodded, her face equally serious. She did see the difference.

"This is so spooky," Maggie said in a loud whisper as they walked through a tumbledown corridor to a small locked room. "Did you see that guy lurking around the corner? I think he's following us!"

Aunt Carla laughed aloud.

"Shh!" Maggie hushed her. "He'll hear you!"

They stopped at the barred door and peered in at the gloomy little room.

"This must be the *jail*," Maggie whispered dramatically.

"Mm-hmm," Aunt Carla agreed.

Suddenly Maggie gasped and clutched her aunt's arm. "What was that?"

"I didn't hear anything," her aunt replied.

"I did," Maggie said emphatically. "It was a quiet footstep. I think that guy is sneaking up on us and is going to try to grab us and push us into the jail!"

Now Aunt Carla really laughed. "Come on, Maggie," she said. "Let's get you and your wild imagination out into the sunshine."

"I do feel better out here," Maggie said as they crossed the green grass of the courtyard. She inspected her arms. "My goose bumps are gone…at least until we get back to that bridge!"

HEROES OF THE FAITH

(Hebrews 11)

Noah built a wooden ark,
Rahab hid the spies,
And Abram offered up his son—
By God their faith was tried.

Moses left the pharaoh's court;
Israel crossed the sea,
And Sarah, withered, old, and frail,
A son at last received.

Israel marched till walls fell down;
Samson stole the gates,
And Gideon, with three hundred men,
The victory did take.

By faith the lions' mouths were stopped;
Faith quenched fire's heat;
By faith the dead were raised to life;
Faith made the foe retreat.

All heroes of the faith were these,
David, Samuel too—
All waiting for the Promised One
Who would their hearts renew.

We are not waiting for His birth,
But still by faith must live:
Looking back to Calvary's cross
Where Christ His life did give.

8. Second Chances

Boing! Boing! Laughter from the neighbor kids floated through the hedge as they jumped on their trampoline, a slippery twelve feet of taut black energy, misted with the morning dew. Tirza and Jaden sat on the bottom step of the deck. In her mind's eye, the girl could see the legs stretching, bodies twirling, and hair bouncing. If only it were she and her brother, Jaden, leaping and tumbling in their own backyard. But all chances of that had been spoiled last night as the promise of a trampoline had evaporated like the morning mist. Last night's conversation played through her mind again and again.

"But Mom!" she and Jaden had protested. "Last year you and Dad said we'd get a trampoline this summer!"

Mom shook her head slowly. "I know it's a big disappointment," she said, "but since Dad's hours have been cut at work, there's no money for that."

Mom sighed as a scowl settled across Tirza's brow. "Now listen," she said. "Since all of Aunt Lisa's kids are grown, she said we can have her trampoline."

"But Mom," Jaden complained, "it's a really old trampoline. It's probably all wrecked."

"Aunty Lisa said there is just a small tear on one side by the springs," Mom told them, "and it's been duct-taped. It's only a half size but will still hold you children, just no adults—"

"Half size!" Tirza's pout became an angry exclamation. "That's not what you and Dad promised!"

"And we still intend to keep the promise," Mom said firmly, "but you know we can't right now…"

Jaden shrugged, but Tirza's stubborn silence met Mom's words, until at last Mom said, "Well, then. I'll let Aunt Lisa know you're not interested."

Squinting into the morning sun, Tirza kicked at a pinecone on the sidewalk—so now there would be no trampoline, new or used, large or small.

Boing! Boing! She listened as the neighbor children's shouts echoed through the silent neighborhood. How she ached to be on a trampoline, doing the flips and double somersaults she was sure she could learn if only given the chance. It was a golden Saturday morning; the air was fresh and chilly, but the bright ball of sun was already sending its warmth through their sweatshirts. She and Jaden should have been biking or swinging on the tire swing before Dad came out and gave them some yard work to do, but, instead, they just sat there—sulking, as Mom would have put it. The only thing they wanted to do was bounce…

Jaden sighed and got up. Tirza watched as he headed over to the shed. She also got to her feet, giving the pinecone one final kick. She shrugged as it landed in the flowerpot. *It just isn't fair,* she thought.

⟶ ⟵⟶ ⟵

"Come up to the deck for a snack!" Mom's voice carried across the backyard to where the kids were pulling weeds in the vegetable garden. Jaden had finished the watering and was helping Tirza weed the last row.

"Just a minute!" he called back to Mom. "We're almost done."

"Bring me a cookie, will you?" Tirza asked Jaden. "I want to sit in the shade by the sandbox."

"It's not *that* hot out," Jaden said. "Wait till summer is really here!" But he went to get their snacks.

Settling himself on their little brother's tricycle, Jaden gulped down his juice before picking up his huge oatmeal raisin cookie.

"Mom said Nick and Sarah are getting Aunt Lisa's old trampoline," he told Tirza around a big bite of cookie.

"What?" Tirza shot up straighter on her perch on the sandbox edge and nearly slipped right in.

"What's the big deal?" Jaden asked. "We didn't want it anyway."

Tirza slumped back down with a look of disgust but didn't answer.

"Hey!" Jaden persisted. "You said it was too small."

"Yeah, but it would've been better than nothing," she finally admitted.

Her brother rolled his eyes and shook his head. "You always want the best," he said, "and now you've got nothing."

"So? You wanted the big one too! Besides, Mom and Dad promised!"

"I know," Jaden agreed, "but I'm just saying we could've at least had a small trampoline if we hadn't been so stubborn."

Now it was her turn to roll her eyes, but inside Tirza knew he was right. Finishing her juice, she climbed into the hammock to eat her cookie.

A cloud mass rolled by in the sky—the big fluffy clouds of summer—promising no rain but just a few minutes of shade. Tirza rolled onto her stomach. Slowly she felt herself relax as the warm sun beat onto her back. The sound of a lawn mower droned in the distance, and the faint smell of freshly mown grass drifted on the breeze.

"If feels like the first day of summer," Tirza said.

"It almost is!" Jaden exclaimed. "Nine and a half more days of school!"

Tirza smiled her pleasure and watched as Jaden dropped a crumb on the sandbox edge for a passing ant. Eagerly it picked up the crumb and scurried off. Soon a few more ants were at the site, and Jaden broke off a few more crumbs, each one bigger than the last. "Let's see what they can carry!" he said with a grin.

The two watched as a small ant hurried right past a cookie crumb to tackle a larger chunk of cookie. Scurrying up one side and down the other, it seemed to be figuring out the best way to carry it.

"Don't be so greedy!" Jaden warned the little ant, and Tirza laughed. But the small ant struggled on, without success. It wasn't long before a far larger ant scooped up the chunk and hurried away.

"Now you've done it!" Jaden exclaimed, popping the last bite into his mouth. The small ant retraced its steps to where the smaller crumbs had lain, but not a single crumb could be found.

"Aw!" Tirza exclaimed in sympathy. "Why didn't you save it a crumb?"

"Nope!" Jaden said cheerfully. He stood up and brushed the crumbs from his hands. "It had to learn the hard way not to be so greedy."

Just then Dad came by on his way to the shed for the weed trimmer. "Ready to cut the grass?" he asked Jaden.

"Yup," Jaden answered.

"Good," Dad replied before turning his attention to Tirza. "If you could quickly pick up the kids' toys and any sticks you find, that would be great," he told her.

"Sure," she agreed. "That's fine."

Finished clearing the yard, Tirza gave her little sister a few pushes on the swing and helped her younger brother dig a hole in the sandbox with his backhoe. They dug too deep and hit dirt, but he didn't seem to mind.

"Okay, buddy," Tirza said as she stood. "It looks good! I'm just going to wash my hands now."

———————

The bathroom felt dim and cool after the bright sunshine outdoors. Swishing the cool water over her hands, Tirza looked at the face staring back at her from the mirror. She thought again of the little ant that had missed out on all the crumbs. *Am I really as foolish as the ant?* she wondered.

She knew she could be stubborn at times. For as long as she could remember, her dad had warned, "Stop being so stubborn about it, Tirza!" But to insist on what she thought was right was ingrained in her very character. Often it cost her dearly, when she recognized her own foolishness too late.

"Stop," Dad had said. *But how?* Tirza felt so helpless as she considered her character. Her dad couldn't change her, and neither could she change herself. Tears pricked her eyes as she rubbed soap between her hands and then rinsed them off.

Hanging the towel back up, she hesitated for a moment in the doorway, then turned down the hall to her bedroom instead of heading right back outside. Her frustration and weakness overwhelmed her, and as her need pressed against her heart an urgent cry rose to Tirza's lips. She could pour out her foolishness to the Lord. From God she could ask for wisdom, for a new nature.

Tirza closed the door to her bedroom. Once again she had spoiled things with her selfish stubbornness, but the Lord had said, "Ask, and it shall be given you.... For every one that asketh receiveth" (Matthew 7:7–8). Each day, she could ask again. With Him there was always another chance.

<hr>

Walking into the kitchen with a lighter step, Tirza found Mom at the stove. "Can we eat outside," she asked eagerly, "on the picnic table?"

"Sure," Mom agreed, "if you will carry the plates and cups outside."

That was quickly done. Then the cheesy goodness of a grilled cheese sandwich topped with juicy tomato and crisp bacon made her mouth water. Despite how sulky she had been, Mom had made her favorite.

"Grilled cheese!" her little brother exclaimed. "Yum!" And he picked some melted cheese off the edge of a sandwich.

Before the meal ended, Dad picked up the Bible to read together. They were reading from the book of 1 Kings, and today's piece told the history of King Rehoboam. At his father's death, the citizens of Rehoboam's country had asked for a break from the heavy burden of the tax money they had to pay the king. Before answering either way, Rehoboam told the people to give him three days to decide. He then asked counsel from his royal court: the aged advisors told him to yield to the people in this matter and they would yield to him for the rest of his life. But the young men who had grown up with Rehoboam advised him to deal harshly with the people to let them know he was in charge.

It was a pity that Rehoboam followed the foolish advice of his friends. The citizens of his country rebelled and chose a new king to rule over them. Only the tribe of Judah remained loyal to Rehoboam, and he lost over three-quarters of his people and land. And because of the divided kingdom, the country would be torn by civil war for generations to come.

"That wasn't very smart," Tirza reflected as Dad finished reading. "Rehoboam was so greedy for more money that he nearly lost it all!"

Dad nodded thoughtfully. "That's right," he said. But in the silence that followed his words, Tirza thought of herself.

It seemed that Jaden did too. He didn't say anything, but Tirza could guess his thoughts as he glanced at her across the table: *Yeah, lost it all like some other stubborn people I know.*

Tirza shrugged and then smiled sheepishly at her brother. "Well, at least we just lost a trampoline, not a kingdom!" she said.

"That's right, Your Highness," Jaden said with a grin. Even Mom smiled.

Dad set aside the Bible, and the family bowed their heads for prayer. It was a relief to Tirza that the discussion about the trampoline was over. There had been no second chance, either for her or for King Rehoboam, but what a blessing it was that with the Lord there was always an open door.

BLESSINGS FROM ABOVE

The little ant runs back and forth
Across the deck below.
It finds the cookie crumbs the boy
Has spilled, but doesn't know
It was his hand that dropped them there—
And, so, no thanks it shows.

We too find blessings from the Lord
Rained down on us below;
We cannot see the One who gives,
But from His Word we know
Whose hand has showered us with good.
He loves the thanks we show.

9. French for Rachel

"I want to have French class! I want to do project too!" Rachel stopped in the doorway of the sixth grade classroom, refusing to budge.

"Come along, Rachel," Mrs. Hilton, the special education teacher, said kindly. "We need this time for your writing lessons."

"Come on! I want to *stay*," Rachel said defiantly, even as her feet reluctantly trailed Mrs. Hilton's down to their own small study room.

During library period, Rachel slipped back into the sixth-grade classroom to speak with the French teacher.

"Can I have French book?" she asked, leaning her round tummy against the teacher's desk.

Miss Catan smiled at the request and got up. "Let me see if we have an extra copy. Hmmm, no, I'm sorry. I don't have any extra textbooks this year, Rachel."

"All right," Rachel answered, looking down at the desk. "I ask libe—libarian."

In the library she approached the librarian for a French book. "I hafta learn French," she explained eagerly, bouncing on the heels of her feet. "The—the kids are doing a project on Monday," she continued, wrinkling her small nose to push up her glasses. "I do a project too."

Rachel waited impatiently for the librarian's response. "Oohhh!" she moaned in frustration as the librarian explained that the only picture dictionary had been checked out. Head down, she trudged on short legs back to class.

Passing her locker, Rachel saw two of her classmates. One of them, Kristen, was holding a picture dictionary. It had the word "FRENCH" written across the cover in large letters.

"You have French book?" Rachel approached the girl a little hesitantly.

"Yeah, I'm getting it out for my little sister."

"Can I have it, bring it home? I bring back tomorrow," Rachel asked hopefully.

Kristen giggled. "Why? You like French?" she asked with a smirk. "You want to learn to talk French?"

"Yeah!" A smile lit Rachel's face, almost closing her almond-shaped eyes. "I be French teacher when I grow up."

At that, Kristen laughed out loud, then covered her mouth. "Here. You better study hard!"

Rachel giggled along with her. "I will," she promised readily and hopped up and down, hugging the book to her chest. "Sank-you, Kristen."

Kristen turned to Caitlin and rolled her eyes. "I don't think she has a clue what goes on at school. Why do her parents even send her here?"

"She's actually very smart," Caitlin answered, grabbing her science book from her locker. "Just because she has Down syndrome doesn't mean she can't learn anything. It just takes her a little longer."

That afternoon, Rachel hurried off the school bus to get started on her project. With a pad of paper and pencil in hand, she began choosing objects to trace from the picture dictionary.

"I do this one and this one," she decided aloud. "I make good project. I love projects. I love French."

After supper, Rachel got out her markers and carefully outlined each object in bright colors. Holding up a girl with pink hair, she giggled. "I like that one. Is my favorite."

On Saturday morning Mom asked Rachel if she would like to go sledding with the neighbor kids.

"No, I hafta finish my French project," Rachel told her as she climbed up onto the chair at her desk. "Mon–Monday is the projects."

Using a pencil, Rachel carefully copied, letter by letter, the name of each object onto the back of its page. Then, stacking the papers together loosely, she stapled them into a booklet.

"All right, Mom!" she called. "I'm done my project now." And she tucked the booklet into her schoolbag for Monday. "There. Now don't forget project," she told herself.

Monday morning, Rachel hurried into school. "See my project?" she showed the kindergarten teacher.

"I made a project," she told the principal.

At her hook, she waved her project in the air to show the other kids.

"Oh boy," Kristen said and nudged Caitlin. "Rachel's made a French project too! Coloring pages, no doubt."

Rachel caught Kristen's eye and smiled happily. Carefully she placed her project on the shelf and hung her coat below. Just then the boy next to her tossed his lunch bag onto the shelf, knocking her project off. It landed on the hall floor in a puddle of melted snow.

"Oops," he said, and, picking up the dripping booklet, put it back on the shelf. "Sorry about that."

Kristen watched silently from her own hook.

"My project!" Rachel cried out. "Is all wet! You wrecked it. Oohhh!" and with a cry of frustration she buried her face in the jackets among the hooks.

Kristen stopped at Rachel's hook on her way into class. "Don't worry, Rachel," she said with a half sympathetic smile. "The teacher won't be mad; you didn't really have to do a project for French."

Rachel raised a tear-stained face and picked up her soggy booklet. "My project," she wailed again, "is all wrecked!"

The look on Rachel's face wiped the smile from Kristen's. She paused, hesitating. "You can make another one," she finally suggested.

"No-o-o," Rachel cried and stamped her foot. "Projects are today! I hafta do it."

Kristen stared for one more moment at the determined face, then held out her hand. "Here," she said. "I'll put your project on the heat register. It should dry in no time."

"Dry on the register?" Rachel repeated, peering up at Kristen over her glasses. "Sank-you." And in a moment her tears had gone as she handed over the project and bent double to peel off her boots.

<hr/>

French class came at last. Rachel clutched a dry and somewhat wrinkly booklet tightly in both hands as she waited for her turn to present.

"Rachel?" came Miss Catan's voice from the front of the room.

Slowly Rachel stood up. A gap-toothed smile lit her face as she walked slowly up the aisle. Her smile widened as she passed Kristen's desk, and she patted the booklet to show her it was really dry.

But as Rachel passed two boys, they began to giggle. Immediately her face fell, and she stopped in her tracks. *Why they laugh at me?* she wondered. Her shoulders drew up in discomfort, and she appeared nervous for the first time.

"It's all right. Come on up, Rachel," Miss Catan encouraged from the front. The giggling stopped as the boys looked up to see what was going on.

"Come on, Rachel," Kristen encouraged from her seat. "No one's laughing at you. Go teach us some French."

"No!" Rachel giggled shyly. "I not a teacher."

"Sure you are!" Kristen said. "You are for today."

Again Rachel looked over the class. Rows of expectant faces smiled back at her. For a moment she turned and peered over her shoulder at Mrs. Hilton. Another nod and smile urged her on.

Rachel took a deep breath. *I go do project,* she told herself. *I teach the kids French.* And holding her booklet out in front of her with two hands, she continued up the aisle to the front of the classroom. All trace of a smile disappeared from her face as she stood behind the lectern.

"Okay, class," she pronounced with authority. "Time for French. Say your words." Then, page by page, she held up the French vocabulary pictures as the students recited them in unison.

For one glorious, shining moment, Rachel was living her dream. She was the French teacher.

PLANNED WITH CARE

(Psalm 139:13–18)

You may be strong, have eyes that see
And legs that shimmy up a tree—
Or maybe legs that cannot walk,
Or you may find it hard to talk.
We all have souls, though, that can love
Our moms and dads and God above—
Don't wish yourself away.

Your shape was planned and drawn with care
By God, who numbers every hair—
Don't wish yourself away.

He doesn't only love the bright,
Those swift ones always in the light,
But sees the beauty of a soul
That loves Him and will soon be whole—
Praising Him with perfect love
Eternally in heaven above—
Joined, at last, with body strong
And lips to sing a brand new song!

10. The Swindler

"Happy birthday, Nicholas!"

Rob's eyes narrowed in envy as his younger brother pulled a shiny new pocketknife from its wrappings.

"Wow! Thanks, Mom and Dad!" Nicholas exclaimed. "Isn't it neat?" he asked, turning to show his big brother the different blades and tools all tucked into one handle.

Rob shrugged. "It's alright," he said and stood still, resisting the urge to reach out and try the different blades. His thoughts were whirling. The things he could do with a knife like that! It would be perfect for shaving bark off branches to make arrows or to carve his name in his tree fort. If he ever got lost in the woods, survival would be right there in his pocket with a knife like that. And if he were ever taken hostage, escape would be right there with all the tools in the knife. *Why have Mom and Dad never given me a knife like that for my birthday?* Rob scowled as he pushed back his chair from the table. Well, it didn't really matter. Before the week was over, the knife would be his.

Rob headed straight to the woods after school. He was meeting the neighbor boy, Calvin, there. They were making a railing for the second story of Rob's tree fort. Having nailed in some upright supports, they were weaving thin branches between them. This would serve a double purpose, for it would give them something to hide behind when the enemy attacked. But it was hard work breaking off the necessary branches, for the fresh green insides would bend but not break.

"If only I had a knife," Rob muttered to himself.

"Rob!" His brother's voice rang through the trees. Before Rob answered, Nicholas was crossing the creek and hurrying up the wooded hill.

"What do you want?" Rob called as his brother came into sight.

"I want to play with you guys," Nicholas answered. "I brought my knife, and we can cut some stuff with it."

"Nah, we don't need it," Rob replied. "Just go on home and play cowboys and Indians with the girls in the backyard."

"What do you mean?" Nicholas asked.

Rob laughed. "You see that little knife you got in your pocket? Just because you're carrying that around, you suddenly think you're something. You think you belong here in the woods. That you're tough and brave."

"No, I don't," Nicholas protested. "I just want to help build the fort."

"Whatever, Nick," Rob said before turning around to keep building. "You just go on home and play with your new toy in the backyard."

"Yeah," Calvin added in a tough voice. "Everything a woodsman needs is right here at our fingertips in the woods. We don't need cheap gadgets like that."

Nicholas knew when he was defeated. Pocketing the knife, he left.

The next day Nicholas stayed in the backyard with his knife. He shaved a bit of bark from a stick and poked the various blades into a hole in the maple tree. Then he snapped the blades shut. What could he really do with a knife in the backyard? His thoughts were with the older boys at their fort in the woods. Stuffing the knife into a crevice in the tree, he ran determinedly to the woods.

"I left the knife at home," he called breathlessly at the tree fort. "Now can I come up?"

The older boys frowned. "No," Rob said carelessly. "You still think you're somebody special 'cause you have a knife."

"Well, what do you want me to do?" Nicholas asked in desperation. "I can't help it I got it for my birthday!"

Silently, his brother held out his hand.

Nicholas's eyebrows rose. "I have to give it to you? What? For how long?"

"For forever!" Calvin said loudly. And the two boys turned back to their work.

Nicholas frowned and turned slowly away. Then, his mind made up, he started jogging for home.

"It's a deal then," Rob said when Nicholas returned. The two brothers shook hands. It had always been this way.

Rob looked stern and serious as he tucked the knife into his own pocket. Then he turned quickly away to hide the thrill of possession that welled up inside him.

Now Nicholas had his brother back—the one who had taught him to swim in the creek, to make a bow and arrow; the brother who had stood up for him against a bully at school and could make him laugh himself sick with stories about the crazy cow on Uncle Ben's farm.

Whistling cheerfully, Rob taught Nicholas everything he knew about roughing it in the woods. Nicholas was thrilled to be included in the older boys' work.

The light was dim in the bedroom that night, but from his bed Nicholas could still see the knife shining brightly on his brother's night table. He almost wished he could ask for it back, but he knew his brother would never give it up. A deal was a deal. Nicholas rolled over to face the wall. Being able to play with the older boys in the woods was worth it; their friendship was worth more than a knife. After all, what could he really do with a knife? He wasn't a city slicker. Everything a woodsman needed was right there at his fingertips in the woods.

When Mom found out about the deal, she spoke up. "Rob, you need to give that knife right back to your brother."

When Rob didn't answer, Nicholas quickly replied, "It's okay, Mom. We made a deal. Rob didn't make me give him the knife. I wanted to."

Mom shook her head. "It isn't right," she said, and then was silent.

A twinge of guilt rose up in Rob's conscience, but he shoved it aside. He *hadn't* taken the knife, he argued inwardly. As Nick had said, it was a deal.

The church service had ended, and Rob had joined the senior class for their Sunday school lesson. The teacher was quizzing them on the story of Jacob and Esau. Rob had always admired Esau. Like Rob, he was the oldest son, and a strong outdoorsman who hunted for a living. Jacob, on the other hand, thought Rob, mostly sat around watching sheep and cooking up soup and schemes against his brother. Remember the nasty trick he had played on his brother?

Rob could well imagine how hot and tired and hungry Esau must have been after a hunting expedition. His own stomach was often growling by the time he came in from the woods after school. And, boy, didn't supper smell good then? But Jacob, that sly brother, had used his tasty cooking to trick Esau out of his rights as the oldest son! Esau was boiling mad when he found out what he had lost.

Rob shook his head. He could just imagine how that must have felt! It was bad enough that he didn't always get what he deserved in the first place as the oldest son—for instance, a pocketknife. But to have been tricked out of it? Rob shifted in his chair, and the knife, which went with him everywhere, pressed against his leg. Rob froze. *Tricked out of it…?* The thought echoed again in his mind. *Like Jacob tricked Esau?* The questions kept coming. *Like he had tricked Nicholas?* Suddenly Rob didn't see himself as the hardworking woodsman, but as the scheming Jacob.

And suddenly Rob didn't find the story so comfortable anymore. Esau had become furious and waited for his chance for revenge. Jacob had to flee for his life. While the brothers did eventually forgive one another, they had never lived together again. Rob swallowed hard. He wished the Bible lesson were over.

Rob tossed and turned on his bed that night. Even with his eyes closed, he could picture the shiny pocketknife on his night table. Other pictures also passed before his mind's eye: the sight of Nicholas trudging away from the tree fort, unwelcome; the sight of Nick's face as he handed over the pocketknife; the happiness on his brother's face at being included in the older boys' fun in the woods. *How mean he had been!* For the first time Rob couldn't push the thought away. The pictures played before his eyes, and sleep would not come as his conscience had its say. The numbers on the alarm clock changed one by one, until at last the guilt became too great. Tears welled up in Rob's eyes as he confessed his guilt before the Lord. Rolling over, he flicked on the light and lightly shook his younger brother.

"I'm sorry I tricked you out of your knife," Rob said as he pressed the knife into Nick's hand.

Nick seemed dazed. "Are you sure I can have it back?" he asked in sleepy surprise. "It was a deal."

"No, it's yours," Rob said.

"And can I still play with you in the woods?"

Rob winced. No wonder Nick had asked; Rob had always been so selfish in the past. "Of course," Rob said aloud. The light shone briefly on Nick as he tucked his birthday present under his pillow before Rob flicked it off. He smiled as a load lifted from his chest.

"Good night, Nick," he said.

"Good night," his younger brother said.

Rob sighed peacefully. By God's grace, his scheming and tricks would not separate the brothers as Jacob's had.

TANGLED IN SIN

I'd like to be a little lamb
Out in the field, I think.
I'd run and leap through pastures green,
Pause at the stream to drink.

There'd be so much to hear and see
That I could play all day
Down in the valley, on the hills—
I'd wander every way.

But trouble I might also find,
For, being just a lamb,
I couldn't save myself from harm
Far from my shepherd's hand.

I might get caught in brambles that
Grow thick and tangled there.

No matter how I'd pull, I'd be
Entangled by my hair.

No effort of my own could save
Me from my foolishness.
My shepherd, only, could undo
The thick and tangled mess.

Though I am not a little lamb
Caught in the thorns out there,
It's sin that catches me and holds
Me fast within its snare.

Just like the little lamb, I cry
For help…and Someone hears:
My Shepherd who can free me from
The sins I hold so dear.

11. Patches's Way

"Can't we get a horse, Dad? Please?" Sophia begged. Mom had rung the dinner bell, and they were coming in from the small barnyard that lay behind the farmhouse. "What's the use of mending the pasture fence if we don't even have any animals to keep in the pasture?" Sophia continued.

"A horse is a lot of work," Dad pointed out. "It's not like getting a new bike."

Sophia sighed, and Dad added, "I'll talk it over with your mom."

"I just can't stand it that we had to move," Sophia complained. "When we lived next to Aunt Jess, I could ride their horses every day after school!" She stomped her foot in frustration. "We just have to get a horse."

"Horses aren't cheap, my girl, and that is why your mom and I will make the decision," Dad said firmly.

"But we have the barn and everything—" Sophia began again.

"That's enough!" Dad said. "Run along into the house and get washed up for dinner."

"Please wait until the bus is stopped, Sophia," the bus driver said as Sophia came hurrying down the aisle.

—71—

"Yeah, yeah," Sophia agreed and dashed down the steps to the road. Swinging her backpack over one shoulder, she stopped short. Far down the long lane she could see movement behind the barnyard fence. It was Dad, and he was leading—could it be—a horse? Throwing her backpack to the ground, the girl took off running. *A horse! A horse!* Her thoughts were running a race with her feet. *Here, right in the barnyard, a horse of my own!*

It felt like a dream.

Dashing down the stairs the next day, Sophia was halfway out the backdoor when Mom's voice stopped her.

"Where are you going in your barn clothes?" she asked.

"I'm going to ride Patches," Sophia answered.

"I know you're excited," Mom said, "but your science report is due in two days, and you still have a lot of work to do on it. I think it would be best to do your homework first—"

"Nah, it'll be fine. I'll do some tonight after supper," the girl called back before letting the screen door bang shut.

Patches tossed his head warily before reaching out long lips to accept the apple from Sophia's hand. He snorted, then sputtered and pranced off to eat it on his own.

"Come back here, you!" Sophia said commandingly to his broad backside. A swish of his tail was his only reply. "You have got to be the sassiest horse I've ever seen," she scolded him. With a *humph!* of her own, she scrambled up the fence and hopped down into the barnyard.

Patches continued to ignore her, shifting only enough to give her the cold shoulder. He wasn't scared, Sophia knew. His ears didn't flatten at her touch, and his eyes didn't widen; he simply moved away.

"Oh, fine!" Sophia stormed. "You don't want to be friends? Well, see if I bring you any more apples." Opening the gate, she went into the barn to get the saddle and bridle.

"Need any help out there?" Dad asked from where he was working.

"I'll be fine," Sophia said. "But that horse simply has the worst attitude of any horse I've ever met," she huffed, as she gathered up a brush and blanket as well. "No wonder you got him for such a good price. He must have been useless as a trail-riding horse."

Dad just laughed.

"The rancher was probably glad to get rid of him!" Sophia finished.

And now he was hers.

Well, she was the boss. It was just a matter of teaching him that, Sophia was sure...but how?

Urging the stubborn creature through the gate, Sophia fit him with the bridle and tied the reins to a fence post. She wasn't taking any chances. Patches didn't seem to mind the brushing and even allowed her to place the light saddle blanket over his back. But when she set out to drape the heavy blanket on top, he resisted, pulling back and jerking his head from side to side. He knew what that blanket meant: a saddle was coming.

"Oh no, you don't," Sophia said through gritted teeth, and, grabbing his reins with one hand, she heaved the blanket on. The saddle followed, and Patches seemed to resign himself to its weight, for he stood quietly as Sophia tightened the cinch.

"There," Sophia said and patted his shoulder. "That wasn't so bad, was it? Now, let's take a little ride, and you can check out the new pasture."

Loosening the reins from the fence, Sophia brought them up over his head and laid them on the nape of his neck. She tucked her feet into the stirrups and swung herself up onto Patches. Clicking her tongue, she urged him on with her feet. "Come on, boy, let's go."

To her surprise, the horse set off in an easy canter, allowing her to guide him. But after a dozen yards or so, he jerked to the right. Before Sophia knew what was happening, the saddle slipped to the side. With a *thump!* she hit the ground, as Patches trotted cheerfully back to the barn.

The girl was more angry than hurt. "So that's the way you play, hey?" she shouted after the retreating horse. "I should have known you would pull that trick."

Sophia had heard of horses that puffed out their bellies while being saddled. Holding air in their stomachs kept the cinch from being tightened properly, and once the rider took a seat the horse would release the air and the saddle would be loose.

Sophia stood and dusted off her pants. "Just you wait," she threatened. "You'll find out soon who's the boss."

⸻

"I can't believe that horse!" Sophia exclaimed. It had taken the dinner bell to bring Sophia out of the barnyard and into the house. She was spending every spare minute she had with her new horse.

"After I figured out his belly trick and got the cinch tightened properly, he wouldn't budge!" the girl continued. "At last I got him moving, but he just ran a tight circle back to the barn. For a horse that is supposed to have a small brain, he knows an awful lot of tricks." She shook her head in frustration as she swirled her fork full of spaghetti.

"Maybe he just has a lot of character," her older brother teased. "That's your standard excuse for going your own way."

"Patrick," Dad said as he poured the drinks. "We don't need to hear that. It does seem like the horse needs a few lessons in submission, though," he agreed.

"That's it!" Sophia said. "That's exactly what I told him. He needs to learn that I'm the boss."

"Well, why don't we take him to the round pen after supper?" Dad suggested. "That's where his training will begin. Because a creature that goes his own way is of no use to anyone."

———

Sophia spent a half hour with Dad and Patches in the round pen. Dad showed her how to hold a whip in her hand and strike the ground with it. The horse was expected to run until the trainer looked down and lowered the whip. As Dad worked with Patches, it quickly became clear that the horse knew what was expected of him but wasn't willing to perform.

"What a stubborn horse!" Sophia sputtered.

"We're all stubborn," Dad said wryly as he walked Patches again around the ring. "How many times do we know what's right, but go wrong? We need training in the school of *God's* discipline!"

"I know, I know," Sophia said. "That's why we study the Bible and learn verses by heart."

Dad nodded. "That's the easier part: memorizing the textbook, the Bible," he said and looked seriously at Sophia. "But what's really in our heart shows during the practical training of daily life."

Sophia didn't answer but watched as he brought Patches over to the gate.

"By the end of his training," Dad explained, "you need to be able to walk away from Patches without looking at him, and he must follow you."

"Let me try it now," Sophia said, holding out her hands for the whip.

"No, I think this fellow has had enough for one day," Dad countered. "Why don't you rub him down, give him a treat, and you can have a go at it tomorrow?"

The sun had slipped beyond the trees, and only the palest of blue lit the sky above.

Still the girl protested. "Aw, come on," she whined. "Just for a few minutes. I want to get the hang of it."

Raising an eyebrow, Dad passed the lead rope into her hand but held onto the whip. "For a girl who's supposed to have a small brain, you know an awful lot of tricks," he said dryly, and headed off toward the house.

Crickets broke the stillness as Dad's footsteps faded away. Sophia stared after him, her mouth open. *Was Dad serious? Am I like Patches? Stubborn and always wanting my own way?*

A heaviness settled over her spirit as the thought dampened her urge to train. She had never before seen herself through anyone else's eyes. *Am I really full of tricks meant for me to get my own way?* the girl wondered. There, in the hush of the gathering dusk, Sophia heard herself for the first time—pestering Dad, making excuses for not listening to Mom, brushing off the bus driver's warnings. *Don't I ever simply obey?* she wondered. And to her shame, she couldn't say she did.

By the time she had rubbed down the horse and given him water and some oats, the stars were coming out. Sophia secured the barn door behind her and headed toward the house. The trill of spring peepers echoed from the pond, and her shoes crunched on the gravel underfoot. It was the kind of night that would ordinarily make one glad to be alive, but Sophia's mind was on other things. Pausing by the training pen, she ran a hand along a rail. Yup, Patches's attitude sure needed some work, but so did hers.

Dad had said it was daily living that showed what was in one's heart, Sophia mused. *And where had he said our training must begin? In the school of God's discipline.* Humbled by the view of her own heart, Sophia knew it was time that she confessed her sinful attitudes to her heavenly Schoolmaster.

THE SADDEST SIGHT TO SEE

An eagle with a broken wing,
A harp without its strings,
A garden overrun with weeds
Are sights so sad to see.

A church that low in ruin lies,
A ship left high and dry…
And, yet, a wayward child may be
The saddest sight to see.

12. Sweeter than Them All

"I can't believe it's raining!" Danielle complained to Chris. "Mom said it was supposed to stop by noon."

Chris frowned in agreement. "It's not fair," he said. "First we couldn't join the tennis class for lessons, and now we can't even go out and play tennis with Dad!"

"Can we please go with you?" Danielle and Chris had pleaded last week. And Dad had agreed. Soon they were waiting in line with Dad to sign up for tennis lessons. Their new rackets lay in the back seat of the car.

"I'm sorry, the class is full," the woman was saying to the boy in front of them.

Chris and Danielle had turned to look at each other in surprise—angry surprise. The twins had not expected this! Sure enough, the woman had spoken the same words to Dad when it was their turn at the table.

Dad had echoed her words on the way to the car. "Sorry kids; we'll have to try again in the spring."

"In the spring!" Chris had exclaimed. "That's half a year away!"

"Well, I'll tell you what," Dad had gone on as they climbed into the car. "I'll take you out to the tennis court in town one night, and we'll get in some practice before then."

But now it was raining.

Forks clattered and pan lids clanged as the family began dinner. "Can you take us to the tennis court tomorrow?" Danielle asked Dad hopefully as she held out her plate.

"It'll probably rain," Chris interrupted around a mouthful of meatball.

"Actually, I have a meeting tomorrow night," Dad told the two. "I should be able to get out there with you next week, though," he added as he picked up his knife and fork.

"Next week!" Chris groaned. *What was the use of a birthday present you couldn't even use?*

———————

The driveway was strewn with crisp brown leaves and acorns from the old oak tree. The blue sky and crisp air promised beautiful weather over the weekend. Danielle raced Chris from the school bus to the house. "Let's practice our tennis on the street," she said breathlessly as they tossed their backpacks onto the porch. "Not many cars come by here."

"Okay, but after our snack," Chris agreed, heading in through the garage. "I'll get the tennis balls."

"Tennis *ball*," Danielle corrected. "We already lost two of them."

THUNK-thunk! THUNK-thunk! It wasn't long before the two were hitting the ball back and forth down the road.

"Let's see how many times we can hit it without missing," Chris suggested. The first few tries were unsuccessful, and they took turns scrambling off the road after the bouncing tennis ball. But soon they were warmed up.

"…nine…ten…eleven!" Chris shouted as he swung wildly for a high shot. *Whack!* The ball sailed smoothly over a neighbor's fence and disappeared into the side yard.

"There goes the last tennis ball," Danielle said in disappointment.

"No problem. I'll get it," Chris assured her as he dashed down the road and leaped over the ditch. Danielle hurried after him.

"What are you waiting for?" she asked her brother as she joined him at the fence. Poking her shoes into the fence holes, she pulled herself up so she could see over it too. "Oh," she said as her eyes caught sight of the orange tabby lying in the grass by the side door. The ball lay between its paws. "It's just a cat," she added.

"Then why don't you get the ball?" Chris asked.

The cat gazed, unblinking, at the two of them.

"No, I'd probably wreck my skirt climbing over the fence," Danielle said.

Chris sighed and climbed higher.

"Wait," Danielle stopped him. "Look by the bush."

Chris looked and saw another cat sitting, unmoving, near a bush. He too had his eyes fixed on the intruders, and as they watched his eyes seemed to narrow into green slits in his black face.

Chris swallowed, took a deep breath, and swung a leg over the fence anyway. But the leg came right back as a third, gray cat came trotting smoothly around the corner of the house.

Danielle was beside him as they leaped back over the muddy ditch to the safety of the road.

"Why would an old lady have so many cats?" Chris muttered as he turned back to stare at the house. "It's creepy." His eyes lit on a green object lying on the front lawn near the road. For a moment he thought it was the tennis ball, but then he realized it was a hard green pear.

Something like a crab apple, he thought. Picking it up, he idly tossed it into the air and whacked it with his racket. To his surprise, it went sailing down the road, nearly to the stop sign at the end.

"Hey, Danielle, watch this!" he exclaimed. And, poking around in the grass beneath the pear tree, he found another. This time he took better aim, and with a great *whack!* sent the pear sailing beyond the stop sign.

"See if you can hit the stop sign," he told Danielle. And soon the two of them were filling the air—and a neighboring yard—with flying pears.

"You did *what*?" Mom asked the twins the next day as she hung up the phone. "Mr. McIntyre called to tell me he can't cut his grass because the lawn is covered with pears…the pears Miss Irma uses for pear sauce!" Mom was digging in the cupboard as she spoke. "Here, take these buckets and get right over there. You can deliver the pears to Miss Irma and explain what happened to them."

The twins had never been so embarrassed in their lives. "It's our own fault," Danielle said as she crawled through the grass looking for pears.

"I guess it was a bad idea," Chris admitted. "But I really don't want to bring these pears to that old lady's house," he added, remembering the cats.

Yet bring them they did, each seeming to walk more slowly than the other. So focused were they on the front door, with the cat staring at them, that they missed the bent figure stooping beneath the pear tree until it straightened. The two jerked in surprise as Miss Irma herself hobbled toward them, also carrying a bucket. Very few pears lay in the bottom of her bucket, however.

"Um, hi," Danielle began after a glance at her silent brother. "We've brought you some pears."

"*Your* pears," Chris corrected.

The old woman looked puzzled.

"We, uh, hit them down the road with our tennis rackets," he explained. He quickly continued as her mouth formed a silent *O*. "We thought they were crab apples—well, crab pears, or something like that. Not really for eating," he stammered.

"And we're sorry," Danielle added, stepping forward with her outstretched bucket. "I hope they aren't too bruised."

At last the woman seemed to understand. "No, no," she said in a small voice. "They should be fine if I peel them all today." She smiled at the children as they set the buckets at her feet. "Do you mind carrying them to the porch?" she asked. "My back isn't as strong as it used to be."

The children breathed a sigh of relief at the woman's mild answer. She had not sounded angry at all!

The gray cat came loping down the steps as the two approached. Chris tensed as it rubbed up against his legs, then relaxed as it let out a vibrating purr.

"Don't mind Whiskers," Miss Irma said. "She's always looking for attention." She turned to open the gate into the side yard. "Go on, Whiskers," she said. "Go join the others."

"I like them to enjoy the sun while they can," she explained. "Winter will soon be here. Now, Ink," she added as a black cat wound its way between her feet, "you stay right there. I'll be along in a moment to peel the pears."

Danielle eyed the two buckets full of pears. It was midafternoon already, and this seemed like a big job to accomplish before nightfall. "Do you need help peeling the pears?" she asked before she could be frightened out of it.

"Oh, well," Miss Irma's words stumbled in surprise. "It *is* a big job, but you should be running home to your mother, I'm sure."

"No, it's okay," Danielle said, ignoring her brother's raised eyebrows. "We can help. After all," she added, looking at Chris, "we are the ones who bruised them."

And so it came to be that a Friday afternoon of tennis led to a Saturday afternoon of pear peeling. But as he sat in the warm sunshine with a cup of hot apple cider and fresh oatmeal raisin cookies, Chris didn't seem to mind. "So, what are this one's bad habits?" he asked, pointing his paring knife at the tabby cat rolling playfully on the patio.

And Miss Irma broke into another cat tale that left the twins grinning.

"There," she said as the last pear joined the others in the large saucepan. "I'll have the sweetest jar of pear sauce for you by Monday night, and not a drop of sugar added," she said proudly.

"Just like her," Danielle said once they were out of earshot.

"What do you mean?" Chris asked as he fell into step beside her on the road.

"The pear sauce is sweet, just like her," Danielle explained. "She's not creepy at all. And neither are her cats."

"I guess," Chris said as he broke into a run. "She sure bakes good cookies. Race you home!"

"No fair!" Danielle called after him. "You left me with both of the buckets!"

But only his laughter drifted back.

TODDAY IS THE DAY

(Hebrews 3:13)

"Later, later," Satan soothes.
"Later you'll have time to pray.
Don't tell God you're sorry now—
Later there'll be time to bow."

When you've spoken words that hurt,
Lied or joked in sinful ways,
When your heart is filled with shame
That you've slandered someone's name,

"Later, later," Satan croons.
"Later you'll have time to pray.
Don't tell God you're sorry now—
Later there'll be time to bow."

Jesus says, "Confess your sin,
Repent, and be washed clean."
Today's the day to hear His voice;
Oh, never make the foolish choice

To push the thought of guilt away
Until a "better" time to pray…
"Later" says the evil one…
But later may not ever come.

13. Too Much Chatter

"Do you think the dirt really is red?" Amanda asked, pressing her nose to the car window. "What makes it red? And why aren't the Prince Edward Island potatoes at the grocery store red? Do they scrub the red dirt—?"

"Hey, look!" she interrupted herself. "There's a hot air balloon!"

"Like you've never seen one of those before," Ryan said dryly from the other side of the back seat. Even with their younger brother, Brad, sitting between them, he couldn't ignore the nonstop questions and comments from his sister.

"Isn't your nose getting flat from squishing it against the window for the last seventeen hours?" he asked.

Amanda seemed to ignore his remarks. "Look!" she continued. "The balloon is above the water—above the ocean. What if it crashed?"

"It wouldn't crash—it would splash," Ryan replied.

"Funny," Amanda answered in a voice that said it wasn't.

"Hebrews 12:14," Dad commented from the front of the car.

"What?" Ryan asked. "We weren't even ready!"

"Well, take out your Bibles," Dad said. "We have time for one more round." The three children scrambled to pull out their Bibles.

Dad knew all kinds of games to play in the car. To help the children learn where the books were found in the Bible, Dad would say a Bible book, chapter, and verse. Whoever found it first would read it aloud and tell what it meant.

Rustling through his pages, Ryan called out triumphantly, "Got it! 'Follow peace with all men, and holiness, without which no man shall see the Lord,' Hebrews 12:14. Um, I guess that means that only people who live peacefully with other people, and who don't live in sin, will one day see the Lord in heaven."

"That's right," Dad said, "and Paul goes on to explain in the next verse that this kind of living will prevent a root of bitterness from growing in your heart and troubling you."

Getting his Bible ready for the next text, Ryan looked out the window, thinking. He really did want to serve the Lord. And he didn't find it hard to live peacefully with most people. But with a sister like Amanda, it was hard not to make sharp remarks, or even think resentful thoughts.

"Oh, boy!" Amanda's shrill voice suddenly interrupted his thoughts. She was peering between the two front seats. "Is that the bridge? It can't be a bridge—it's so long!"

"Yup, that's it," Mom answered from the front seat. "And it looks like it will be a long drive over it, at least ten minutes."

Even Ryan peered ahead at the road that seemed to leave the mainland and jut out seemingly endlessly across the water to the island. "Whoa!" he said. "I wonder how long it took to build this bridge!"

"Now look who's being curious!" Amanda said. "But what did they do before there was a bridge?" she suddenly wanted to know. "Did they take boats across?"

"I'm sure there was a daily ferry," Mom answered. "There have always been people who live on Prince Edward Island but work on the mainland, you know."

———

"I hope, I hope, I hope we see some whales!" Amanda exclaimed, jumping up and down next to the railing.

Ryan sighed. It was their last day on Prince Edward Island, and it had been a week full of Amanda's questions. Now the family had just boarded the ferryboat for a whale-watching tour, and the boat hadn't even left the docking area yet.

"I want to see them spray out their blowhole," Amanda continued. "And I want to get a picture of it," she added, holding up her camera to be ready. Turning to Dad, she asked, "Why do whales spray water out of their blowholes, anyway? Why don't they just breathe air out the way we do?"

"That's a good question," Dad said. "Maybe you'll have to ask the tour guide once we're on our way."

Ryan raised his eyebrows. "The poor tour guide," he started to say, but bit his tongue. *Live peaceably,* he told himself. *Ignore her constant chatter.*

———

"If you'll turn and look to the rear of the boat, you'll see we have some visitors."

Most tourists had left the rails by now and were relaxing in the warm sun. At the tour guide's voice, however, many got up and hurried to the back of the boat.

Amanda and Ryan were the first ones there. "Dolphins!" Amanda exclaimed.

"Porpoises," Ryan corrected her. "We learned about them at school. Look, why don't you stand over there," he suggested, pointing to an empty spot at the other rail. "You'll be able to see better." *And I'll be able to hear better,* he thought unkindly.

"Okay," Amanda agreed cheerfully. "I want to get a picture of the dolphins!"

"Porpoises!" Ryan corrected and turned back to the rail. *At last, some peace and quiet.*

"Actually," the man next to him spoke as he put down his binoculars. "Actually, dolphins are from the larger family of sea creatures called porpoises."

"Oh," Ryan said meekly.

"That your sister?" the man continued. At Ryan's nod, he went on. "It's nice to have brothers and sisters close in age to you. Other friendships fade, but family will be your friends for life."

Ryan raised his eyebrows. His expression showed his doubt. "Did *you* have any brothers or sisters?" he asked.

"Two brothers and one sister," the man replied. "We argued a lot with my sister while growing up. She said we always criticized her. I was just starting to get along with her when she moved to England." He paused before continuing. "She died there in a car accident. I always wished I had appreciated her more while we were growing up."

Ryan didn't know what to say. He was actually glad when Amanda came crowding between them at the rail. "I can get a better picture from here," she said breathlessly. "Look, there's another dolphin—no, porpoise! Whatever!" And she laughed.

For once Ryan was glad for her relaxed and happy chatter. "Did you get any pictures?" he asked.

"Not very good ones," she answered, "because my camera doesn't zoom in."

Ryan hesitated. *Could he be the first one to make things right between them?* Before he could change his mind, he slipped the camera strap from around his own neck. "You can use mine," he offered, "if you're careful."

Amanda's eyes widened in surprise. *The camera he had saved up for? The camera no one was allowed to touch?*

"Thanks!" she said with wonder. "Cool!" she added as she got a closer shot. "Why are they following the boat, anyway?"

Ryan sighed, then smiled. *Here she goes again,* he found himself thinking.

"Do they think we'll feed them?" Amanda persisted. "What do they eat, anyway?"

The man standing next to them laughed, and Amanda turned to him in surprise. "Well, I don't think they are exactly like swans or geese looking for bread handouts," he said, "but if this were a fishing boat, we might get dolphins following us for leftover fish handouts. That's their main diet, you know. An average, 1,100-pound, twelve-foot-long dolphin can eat fifty pounds of fish a day." Seeing he had captured the children's attention, the man continued. "They need the food for energy, for they can travel at speeds of thirty kilometers—that's eighteen miles per hour. Or they can make rapid dives down to more than one thousand feet, or leap out of the water to a height of sixteen feet before landing on their back or side."

"How do you know so much about dolphins?" Amanda asked. "Are you a scientist?"

Ryan cringed in embarrassment. *Would the man think Amanda was rude?*

"No, no," the man answered with a smile. "I'm no scientist, but I do love nature and wildlife. Captain Joe, there, is my brother," he said, gesturing toward the boat's cabin. "I'm retired now, and I often join him on his tours. I love being out on the water."

"Oh, I see," Amanda said before drifting off down the rail to try to get a better picture.

"You like taking pictures?" the man asked Ryan.

"Yeah, I've been trying to get pictures of all kinds of different wildlife. These are the first pictures I have of dolphins."

"Well, they're fascinating creatures, that's for sure," the man said. "They're very intelligent and curious, you know—kind of like your sister!" And he laughed. "They've been known to find underwater objects and carry them to the surface before letting them sink again. But that may also be because they're quite playful. Playful and friendly."

Ryan nodded and watched as the dolphins' gleaming wet bodies flashed through the air, leaving a spray of sparkling water. It looked as though the dolphins were having fun. *"Playful and friendly,"* the man had said. *"And curious."* That did sound like Amanda.

Maybe that was it, Ryan thought. *God wanted him to live peaceably with all people. It would be a lot easier to get along with his sister if he looked for*

the good things in her instead of focusing on what bothered him. After all, didn't he have faults too? Ryan resolved to pray about this.

———————————————

"I can't believe the dirt was really red!" Amanda said brightly as she settled back with a stack of brochures and pamphlets she had picked up over the week.

Ryan gave a mock groan from his side of the backseat. "How many more hours until we're in Ontario?" he asked before jokingly wrapping a pillow over his ears.

"Now look who's being curious!" Amanda said teasingly.

Instead of denying the charge, Ryan shrugged. "Guess you're rubbing off on me," he said.

"Time to study your Bible books," Dad said from the front seat. "Luke 6:41."

The three children quickly pulled out their Bibles. Amanda found it first. "'And why beholdest thou the mote [speck] that is in thy brother's eye, but perceivest not the beam that is in thine own eye?'"

A beam in my eye and only a speck in hers? Ryan thought. *Yeah, I guess I was so focused on her small habit of chattering that I missed my own giant habit of criticism.*

CREATURES OF THE DEEP

(Jonah 1:17; Matthew 17:27; John 21:6)

With a splash of its tail
A mighty whale
Dove deep to swallow Jonah.

With its mouth open wide,
A fish supplied
The coin for Peter's taxes.

With a rush to the net
The fishermen set,
The fish obeyed God's bidding.

If the fish of the sea
Heed God's decree,
Then how much more shouldn't we?

14. Surprised by Joy

The morning air was crisp, telling of ripening apples and farm stands loaded with vegetables, but by noon the temperature felt like summer again. Still, the changing of the season couldn't be mistaken. Instead of the lawn mower, the buzz of a chainsaw rang through the woods. And instead of the croaking of frogs in the pond, the honking of geese rang through the sky.

Maybe Peter didn't notice the way the sun shone golden through the yellowing birch leaves. Maybe he didn't think about the smell of wood smoke drifting lazily on the breeze. But as he bumped along the trail through the woods on his quad, he did know one thing: being outside felt good.

His cousin Dave had come over that Saturday morning, as usual, and they were helping Peter's dad clear some dead trees to be chopped for winter firewood. Dad was working the chainsaw, while Pete and Dave dragged branches out of the way and loaded the little trailer with small logs. Work like this didn't feel like work. The boys would much rather be out in the woods with Dad doing a man's work than hanging around the house. Besides, now that Peter was twelve, Dad let him drive the quad on his own. Back and forth from the woods to the shed, the boys hauled load after load of wood.

Peter wouldn't treasure those fall Saturdays until they were gone. But they were gone, suddenly. It happened on Dave's birthday. The phone rang, and Peter could hardly believe his ears. It was Dave on the other end; he couldn't wait to tell Pete that he had gotten a quad of his own for his birthday. Would Pete like to come over and try it? Would he ever! Dad could spare Peter that afternoon, and Mom said he could bike over to Dave's right after lunch.

So began the Saturday afternoons of quad racing. With such a satisfying rumble of the engine, the quad seemed meant to be raced. The boys would take turns, timing each other as they rode the perimeter of the back field. This was nothing like pulling a trailer of firewood. Here were speed and power, and the exhilaration of taking the bumps and dips along the way.

"They're going to have an accident," Mom said nervously to her sister as the two moms watched the boys from Aunt Teresa's back deck.

"Oh, they'll be alright," Aunt Teresa replied. "Jed said the path is pretty level, and they really can't go all that fast. They always wear their helmets, and they're not allowed to go off the property."

Still, Mom couldn't help being anxious.

◆━━━━━━◆◆━━━━━━◆

There were days when Dave wasn't home, or was busy. Then Peter couldn't go over and ride the new quad with him. On those days he took the old quad into the woods to help Dad, or simply to ride the trails. But it just wasn't the same. Bumping along a trail alone just didn't have the excitement of their races at Dave's. And as he rode, Pete couldn't help seeing the electrical tape wound here and there about the handgrips and seat. He couldn't help feeling how loose the steering was, and how extra bumpy the ride. Comparing this old quad to Dave's was like comparing an old farm horse to a racehorse.

When the novelty of racing wore off at Dave's, Pete thought that maybe they could go exploring with the two quads. Maybe Dad would let him take the old quad over to Dave's place. But Dad said no. The quad was for doing work around the property; it wasn't a toy or a machine for racing.

Mom could see how restless Peter had become. "Why don't you ask Dave over here this Saturday?" she suggested. "You boys used to be busy all day outside, and you never complained."

Peter shrugged, but when Saturday came he really didn't feel like going over to Dave's again to race the quad. After all, only one boy could race at a time, and by now it was getting hard to beat their old records.

"Do you want to come over to our place?" he asked his cousin.

"Sure," said Dave. "I haven't come over for a while."

The boys hooked up the small trailer and took the old quad out to the clearing in the woods, but Dad wasn't cutting firewood that afternoon. They could have collected kindling and brought it back to the shed, but somehow that felt like too much work.

"Let's just go for a ride," Dave suggested.

"Sure," Pete agreed, and he took Dave on the trail that looped through the woods and back home again. Back at the house, they hopped off. Now what? There didn't seem to be anything else to do, and the two hung around the backyard talking.

When Dave headed home, Peter went into the garage. Dad was replacing the blade on the lawn mower.

"Have fun?" Dad asked.

Peter shrugged. "It was alright, I guess," he said.

"What did you do?" Dad asked.

Peter shrugged again. "Not much," he said. The truth was that he couldn't stop imagining what fun they would have had if they could have taken Dave's new quad down the forest trail.

"Pass me the wrench, please." Dad held out his hand, then began tightening the bolts. "The quad ran fine?" he asked.

"Yeah," Pete sighed. "The steering's a little off, and the handlebars vibrate pretty bad, but it's fine for hauling wood."

Dad looked up, surprised. "That new quad of Dave's has spoiled you!" he said. "A few weeks ago I could hardly get the two of you off that old quad, and now it's hardly good enough."

Peter looked down, ashamed. What could he say? What Dad had said was true.

⊷————⊶⊷———⊷

It was while riding home from school the next week that Peter saw a quad for sale. A "FOR SALE" sign was posted next to one of the neighbors' driveways, just down the road from his house.

Peter couldn't believe it. The quad was newer than his dad's old one, and if it were to become his own, wouldn't Dad let him drive it over to Dave's house? Excitement coursed through his body, and, dashing down the steps from the school bus, he raced straight into the house to his room. He had to have a look at his bankbook.

The amount of money he had saved up hadn't changed since the last time he had checked. Still, Peter calculated that if he could do some chores at Uncle Reuben's this month, he might have enough to buy the quad.

———————

"He doesn't need a new quad. It's just coveting."

Peter overheard Mom talking to Dad at the top of the stairs.

"He never even wanted a new one until he saw Dave's!" Mom went on.

Pete hurried to the back door. He didn't want to hear the rest of this conversation, but Dad's words floated out the door after him.

"I know," Dad said to Mom. "I wish Peter could be happy with the old quad like he used to be."

Pete headed out to the shed to get a rake. Dad had told him to rake the leaves from the side yard before dinner. The boy's thoughts flew back and forth with the rake.

I shouldn't have even told Dad and Mom about the quad for sale down the road, he thought. *Even with doing chores at Uncle Reuben's, I might not have enough money. Still, if I do, there will probably be a few weeks yet before any snow falls. I could go over to Dave's place every day after school. But what if Dad doesn't even let me buy the quad? What then?* Mixed feelings of discontent and excitement rose and fell within the boy as he worked his way around the yard.

After supper, Peter took the phone to his room. Written on the back of his hand was the phone number on the "FOR SALE" sign. He had copied it down from the bus window that afternoon. Twice he started dialing, and then quickly hung up.

Come on! Just call! he told himself. And a minute later the phone call was over…as were his hopes and plans. They were asking for way too much money. He would never be able to afford the quad.

Peter flopped down on his bed and rolled over to stare blankly at the wall. An hour passed, and Mom knocked on his door, wondering if he would like to join her for a snack before bed.

"No," Peter answered listlessly. "I'm not hungry." The room had grown dark, but still he lay there on the bed, staring at the ceiling. Tomorrow was Saturday, and he didn't even care. All his hopes were dashed. *What is the fun of being home if there is nothing fun to do?* he thought miserably.

At last he got ready for bed. Out of habit, he brushed his teeth and changed his clothes. Picking up the Bible that sat beside his bed, Peter flipped it open to the bookmark. Last night he had read about King Ahab's battle with the Syrian king Ben-hadad. Tonight's passage was about King Ahab trying to buy a vineyard that he wanted. The king wanted it so badly that when he found out it was not for sale, he was very upset. He may have been the king of Israel, but Peter was surprised to read that Ahab lay down on his bed with his face to the wall and refused to eat.

That's ridiculous! Peter thought, setting down the Bible for a moment. But almost immediately the picture of himself lying on his bed and refusing a snack came to mind. Embarrassed, the boy quickly picked up the Bible and read on. The story did not have a happy ending. King Ahab did get the vineyard he wanted, but an innocent man was murdered for it, and King Ahab himself was told that he would die in the place where that man had died.

Soberly, Peter set down the Bible. He had been acting as selfishly as the wicked king. No, he hadn't had any plans to commit murder or to steal the quad he wanted, but he had let his disappointment spoil his own happiness, as well as his mom's and dad's. Peter was ashamed; he knew he needed to confess his sins to the Lord, who stood ready to forgive.

The Saturday morning air was crisp, rich with the smell of fallen leaves and harvested gardens. Sunlight glowed through the orange leaves of the maple trees, and the scent of wood smoke floated on the breeze.

Maybe Peter didn't notice as he bumped along the trail through the woods on his quad, but he felt light inside. The sin of discontentment had dragged him down. With the heavy weight of wanting a new quad gone, he felt comfortable, relieved, free again to enjoy his work. Sure, the ride on this old friend wasn't nearly as smooth as on Dave's new quad, and the rattling handlebars still bothered him now and then, but Pete knew one thing: having a job to do and a quad to ride while doing it felt surprisingly good.

The buzz of Dad's chainsaw rang through the woods, and Peter headed toward the sound.

MEANTIME

I'd love to sail someday—
Sail around the world!
But meantime I would like to see
Creation and explore
The trees and birds, the stream and bugs
Outside my own back door!

I'd love to build someday—
Build a castle white!
But until then I'll work with sand,
Or fashion my own kite,
Design an igloo in the snow—
Create with all my might!

I'd love to teach someday—
Teach the mind to search
Out everything that's lovely, true.
So meantime I'll find worth
In study that reveals God's work
In man, the past, this earth.

I'd love to paint someday—
Landscape, portrait, frieze!
But until then I'll sketch the birds,
The flowers, houses, trees,
Or paint a card for someone dear…
That's what I'll do—all these!

15. Behind the Backstop

"Hey, Kirsten! Why don't you play baseball instead of sitting on the swings?"

Kirsten gave a little push with her feet while thinking of an answer. But her brother was already gone—gone to join the kids in his class with their baseball game.

Most of the girls from her class were sitting talking on the playground equipment. A few of them had wandered over to the baseball diamond, pushing and giggling until they had been invited to join in the game. Kirsten watched as they struck out or were tagged out at first or second base. Her fingers ached to hold the bat. She could show them…if she only had the courage!

It had all started the second week at school. This year the girls were too old for playing house under the big maple tree or trading stickers at lunch hour. Even jumping rope had fallen by the wayside as the girls simply sat and talked the lunch hour away.

"I can't believe Niccy got an A on her science project," Jess had said as they burst out the doors for recess. "She never does well on projects; I just know her sister did it for her."

Kirsten had frowned before speaking up. Jess wasn't being fair. "Maybe she worked really hard on it this time. And it's not wrong to get some help on the project—especially ideas—as long as the work is yours."

Jess frowned back at Kirsten and then laughed. "Don't you sound just like the teacher?" she said. "Maybe that's what you should become."

Kirsten simply shrugged. Jess was often jealous—everyone knew that.

But Jess wasn't finished. "Speaking of teachers," she said loftily. "I heard Mr. Blackwell plays favorites. His nieces and nephews are the only ones who ever get As."

"Oh, Jess," Kirsten said. "That's just a crazy rumor. I'm sure he doesn't give other A students Bs and Cs."

Jess glared at Kirsten. "Whose side are you on, anyway?" she demanded.

Kirsten only shook her head. "There aren't any *sides*," was what she wanted to say. "We are supposed to love everyone and respect those in authority." But she couldn't get the words out and simply walked away.

Kirsten was never excluded from the group of girls after that, but if a conversation fell silent at her arrival she grew uncomfortable. She couldn't help wondering if they had been talking about her. And so she joined them less and less often and would wander off in search of something else to do.

Back home, Mom reminded her that it was what God thought of her that counted. Kirsten knew this in her head, and even felt sure of it in her heart sometimes, but often it wasn't enough to calm the nervous jitter she felt in her stomach.

Reading her Bible at night, she came across the passage about Elijah on the mountain with the priests of Baal. He had openly challenged the king, priests, and Israelites, and God had given him the victory. How she wished there were something big and brave and daring she could do, something that would impress her classmates forever. Something that would make them admire her and not criticize her for standing up for what was right.

Perhaps there would be a fire, Kirsten let herself daydream, *and I would sound the alarm or rescue a child from the burning building. Or there could be a snowstorm and the bus would slide into the ditch near my house. I would be the only one who could guide the bus driver and the children through the blizzard to safety. Then I would feel confident and the other kids would accept me.*

But reading her Bible that night, Kirsten found that even such a dramatic display hadn't been enough to keep up Elijah's courage. Running away into the wilderness, he had sat down under a tree and asked God to let him die. Kirsten nodded as she read. She knew the feeling of wanting to curl up in her home and not go out each morning to face school.

But an angel had come to strengthen Elijah, Kirsten read on, for God still had work for him to do. She closed the Bible with a sigh. She couldn't stay home either. She had schoolwork to do and classmates to face. Bowing her head, she prayed. She needed to be strengthened as well.

It was the next day, at lunch hour, when her brother called out to her on the swings. No, Kirsten hadn't felt as nervous that day, but she would still rather stay on the swings than join the other girls. There was nothing to talk about, and even if she never played she'd rather watch the baseball game.

That night's Bible reading brought Elijah up onto the mountainside, facing wind and earthquake and fire, all without the presence of God. But after the fire, he heard God address him in a "still small" voice. Kirsten paused. *Didn't she have God's word to listen to, too? And wouldn't the Lord hear her prayers and comfort her with His word through His Holy Spirit?*

Kirsten read further: God said to Elijah, "'Yet I have left me seven thousand in Israel, all the knees which have not bowed unto Baal'" (1 Kings 19:18). *Could there be others in her class who loved the Lord but were afraid to speak up for what their consciences told them?*

She turned back to the story, reading verses 19 and 20. How would things go now for this servant of God? "So he departed thence, and found Elisha…and cast his mantle upon him. And [Elisha] left the oxen, and ran after Elijah."

What an answer! Kirsten thought as she closed the Bible. *The Lord did understand Elijah's trouble and gave him a helper.* "Oh, Lord," she prayed, "I wish I had a friend who would understand."

It was October already when a new girl joined Kirsten's class. Kirsten could imagine how nervous she must be and made sure she greeted her, showed her their lockers, and explained the class schedule. But Penny quickly became comfortable with all their classmates. When Kirsten saw her laughing and talking with those around her at lunchtime, she backed off. Penny didn't need her; she was fitting in just fine with all the other giggling girls.

It was Penny's second week of school, and Kirsten was spending the recess hour perched on top of the monkey bars with a book. Penny came out from the school and, instead of joining the other girls, headed to Kirsten instead.

"Hi," she said, and her smile was wide beneath friendly eyes and a thick shock of bangs. "It gets kind of boring just standing around," she said. "Is that why you're up there?"

Kirsten nodded. She didn't want to admit that she had grown nervous of her classmates. "Yeah," she agreed. "There's not all that much to talk about besides school and homework."

"No, and talking about other people is kind of interesting, but wrong," Penny said. "When I told the other girls that, they said I was starting to sound like you!" she added, and laughed.

Kirsten stared at her in surprise. *How could she laugh about that? Wasn't she hurt or embarrassed?*

"Don't look so surprised," the new girl said as she scrambled up onto the monkey bars beside Kirsten. "Maybe it was a compliment! Besides, it doesn't really matter what they think of me."

"How did you get like this?" Kirsten at last asked as she found her voice. "I mean, how come you're so brave and dare to talk to anyone? I've known all the girls since kindergarten, but I seem to just get more and more nervous about what they think of me, and…I don't know…it's not much fun going to school anymore."

Penny shrugged. "Well, last year I had a teacher who always told us not to worry about what others think. What God thinks of us is what matters."

"My mom says that too," Kirsten said. "But I don't always remember."

Penny looked over Kirsten's shoulder. "Aha," she said. "You're watching baseball. Now *that* is one thing that makes me nervous: someone throwing a hard white ball at me, and I'm only given a long skinny stick to defend myself with!"

Kirsten laughed. "I wish I could play with them," she confided. "It's one sport I know I'm good at."

"You are?" Penny demanded in surprise. "Well, what's stopping you?"

"It's all the boys and the *popular* girls who are playing," Kirsten replied.

"That's crazy," Penny said, and Kirsten yelped as she was shoved off the monkey bars down to the ground below. "Come on," Penny ordered. She jumped down and pulled Kirsten along. "We're going to play baseball."

Kirsten swallowed the lump of fear in her throat, even as she laughed at her bossy new classmate. God had given her a friend!

Smack! The ball went soaring through the air, over the infield, and over the heads of the unsuspecting outfielders. Dust and gravel flew as Kirsten's shoes took off for first base, then second. Planting her toe firmly on the bag, she leaned over, panting. She felt surprise and respect from her classmates, but somehow it didn't mean as much as she had thought it would. She couldn't stop the smile from covering her face, however, for even if she had been tagged out or had struck out at the plate, there was her new friend behind the backstop, jumping up and down, cheering.

Kirsten's gaze lifted beyond the backstop into the endless blue sky as a silent prayer of thanks rose from her heart.

CLOSER THAN A BROTHER

(Proverbs 18:24)

I'll lift you when you've fallen down;
When sad, I'll comfort you.
I'll make you smile instead of frown—
'Cause that's what brothers do.

When things go wrong that I can't right,
I'll tell you of Another;
When I can't help, I'll show a Friend
Who's closer than a brother.

He'll listen when you cry to Him;
He'll hear your every prayer.
He'll help you every day anew;
Your troubles He will share.

He'll be a Friend to all who turn
To Him in earnest prayer.
Repentant of their sins, they'll find
A Friend who's always there.

16. Wait for Me!

"Race you to the dock!" Paul shouted to Tim and Jerome. And the three boys took off, arms and legs pumping, heedless of the rough stones and twigs beneath their bare feet.

"Wait for me!" Ricky called from behind, carrying a towel over his arm. With his shorter legs, he just couldn't keep up.

Paul hesitated mid-stride and glanced back at his brother. He frowned. "Not this time, Ricky! We can only fit three people in a canoe. I'll go with you some other time."

"No! I never get to come with you guys," Ricky panted. "And there's no one else here for me to play with. Wait up!"

But the three boys were already at the dock. Quickly they piled into a canoe and pushed off.

They were headed to the jumping rock, just around the bend in the lake. It was one of their favorite things to do at the cottage. Paul and Tim manned the paddles, while Jerome balanced on a stack of life jackets in the middle of the canoe.

Just once Paul glanced back and saw Ricky scrambling into another canoe. *Silly kid,* he thought. *He will be going in circles, paddling that thing by himself.*

Soon their canoe had rounded the bend, and the boys were tying it up and climbing the rock. A giant water spider came crawling down to meet them, and with a shudder they scrambled past it. Giving a hoist to the first one up, then turning to help the ones below, they all reached the top. There they stood. Who would go first?

It's always that first plunge that makes my heart leap into my throat, Paul thought. *I'm not going first!* He was glad when Tim, with a wild shout and a wilder leap, flung himself from the rock. Out, out into the air he sailed, arms flailing like a windmill. A satisfying *ker-splash!* signaled his landing, and in a moment his face popped above water, grinning madly. "Come on, chickens!" he called.

And so Paul made the leap, and Jerome followed. Soon the boys were inventing games. Who could make a full turn in the air before landing? Who could make the biggest cannonball splash?

Outwardly Paul joined in the fun, but inwardly he could still hear Ricky's "Wait for me!" and see him scrambling into the wobbling canoe…without a life jacket. Paul laughed half-heartedly as the other two gave ringing Indian war whoops all the way down. An uneasy feeling settled in the pit of his stomach. He tried to shake it off. *What's the matter?* Paul asked himself. *If Ricky is still stuck going in circles at the dock, that isn't my problem. He has to realize he can't always tag along with us older boys.*

"Hey!" Jerome called up from the water. "I know what we can do. Let's—"

"I'm heading back for a minute," Paul interrupted suddenly. He could feel the blood rushing to his head as a feeling of dread filled him. His heart began beating more quickly. "You guys wait here," he said. "I'll be right back." And, plugging his nose, he jumped off the rock.

His fingers shook terribly as he tried to untie the knotted rope that secured the canoe to a branch. "Come *on*!" Paul muttered furiously. At last the rope came free, and he leaped into the canoe, teetering wildly. Water sloshed up his arms as he paddled rapidly, first on the left side, then on the right. He was almost at the bend. Then he would be able to see him. *See what?* Paul asked himself. *See Ricky sitting back at the shore on the dock, no doubt.* But his heart told him otherwise.

He heard him before he saw him. A gurgle and a watery shout. "Pa-ul! glub—glub—"

Two long pulls of the paddle brought Paul around the bend. Then he saw it. The canoe floating upside down, and a small white face trying to stay above water. Thin arms were desperately grasping and slipping off the smooth sides of the canoe. Ricky could swim without a life jacket, but how long had he been struggling there?

"Ricky!" Paul gave a hoarse shout. "Hang on!" Fear doubled his efforts, and the canoe seemed to surge forward. In a moment he was at his brother's side. Kneeling in the front of the canoe, he reached forward and grabbed for Ricky's flailing arms. On the third try he caught one and brought the panicked fingers to the canoe's edge. The canoe dipped dangerously to the side but stayed just above the surface as Paul began inching back to the cottage shoreline.

As for Ricky, the exhausted boy could do no more than clutch the canoe's edge and be pulled along, his trusting eyes never leaving Paul's face.

At last the canoe hit bottom, and with a gulp Paul grasped Ricky under the arms and pulled him up the sandy beach. And there they stayed, slumped in the sand. Ricky would not let go of his brother's arms, and Paul could not.

"I knew you'd come," Ricky murmured through chattering teeth.

Paul hung his head. He almost hadn't. And yet, a prayer of thanks rose in his heart. By God's grace, he had come.

TO SERVE HIS WAY

(Matthew 26:39; Romans 8:32)

To think of others first is hard,
Especially when they
Don't think of what you want at all
But always want *their* way.

Sometimes it makes you burn inside—
Your face gets hot and red.
"They don't deserve my kindness, so
I'll have my way instead."

But there was One who spent His days
In helping those who cried
For Him to come and heal their wounds—
Not one did He deny.

It mattered not how tired He was,
How sore His feet or voice;
He always put the others first—
That was His Father's choice.

He asked once for another way—
The cross loomed up ahead—
Yet "Not my will, but thine be done"
Was what He finally said.

He gave His life! So won't He grant
Our daily prayers for love?
It is His joy to fill our hearts—
Reflecting His above.

17. Missing!

The cousins were over, making the old house ring and shake with laughter and running feet. When lunch was finished, Emily had taken them out to the barn to see the few sheep that weren't out to pasture. After trying to pet the frisky lambs, the cousins had played in the haymow. It was mostly empty, except for a few bales of hay and a new litter of puppies. The puppies, of course, were the best part. They looked just like their mother, with thick, creamy-white hair and brown eyes. Maremmas made excellent sheep dogs, and Emily's dad kept a few of them to keep watch over the sheep in the pasture. Loyal and protective, the large dogs would keep any coyotes from crossing the fence line.

Emily loved the dogs. Polar was head of the pack. He was the oldest and wisest, and Dad relied on him the most. The puppies, however, acted as all puppies do. Frisky and playful, they climbed over one another and nipped at the children's hands.

The children had just come in for hot chocolate when Dad stood up from the table.

"I've just got to check the fence line before dark," he said, as he set down his empty coffee cup. "I saw coyote tracks around the fence this morning, and I'm going to leave the dogs out there overnight."

Emily's uncle stood too. "I'll come with you," he said. "That way the women will have room to get supper ready!"

The cousins, of course, wanted to come too.

"That should be fine," said Dad. "You can come as far as the pasture."

Emily called Polar from the barn, and they were off. The children ran ahead, their breath making frosty puffs of air against the red, sinking sun.

"Last one to the bridge is the rotten egg!" one of the boys called, and the children ran even faster. They arrived at the pasture laughing and out of breath. Winter was near, but the light snow hadn't covered the long grasses of the meadow yet, and the cousins could see the sheep that were still let out to pasture. Emily let Polar into the fenced area with the sheep, as the cousins looked around curiously.

The pastureland rolled away in every direction, with fences running up and down the steep hillsides.

"That's a nice pond down there!" one of the girls exclaimed. "Maybe when it gets colder we could come over and go skating!"

Emily smiled. "That would be fun," she said. "But we usually have to shovel all the snow off first."

Just then the men caught up with the children. "You kids can run on back to the house now," Dad said. "It'll be dark soon, and supper will be ready."

The children headed back slowly, tired from their earlier race, but Emily's eyes sparkled. No one had noticed her walking quietly behind the others, and she thought it would be fun to cut across the pasture and beat them to the barn. She would jump out and scare them as they passed.

The route across the hills was a little longer, but Emily was sure that if she ran she could beat her cousins to the barn. There was no danger of getting lost in these hills that all looked the same, for Emily spent her summer days out here with Dad, moving the fences and riding the old brown mare. She knew the pastureland as well as her own front yard.

Emily's cheeks glowed as she jogged steadily up one small hill, then up the next. She felt warm from the exertion and loosened her scarf. She was just running along the tree line when it happened. Passing an old tree stump, her foot broke through the long crusty grasses and slipped down into a groundhog hole.

One moment Emily was upright, and the next she was flat on her belly with her leg twisted under her. Quickly she yanked her foot up but cried out in pain. Her lower leg felt bruised, and a sharp pain shot through her ankle when she tried to move her foot.

"Ow!" Emily cried softly to herself and covered her face. Taking a deep breath, she used her good leg to push herself up against the tree stump. Gingerly she tried to put weight on the twisted ankle. She would have to hobble home somehow. It was beginning to grow dark.

⁂

It wasn't until everyone sat down for supper that one of the children asked, "Where's Emily?"

Everyone looked around the table. Where *was* Emily? Hadn't she come back with the cousins from the pasture? Who had seen her last?

Dad stood up as quickly as he had sat down. "She knew we were going to eat soon," he said seriously. He looked at his watch. "I sent the kids back to the house nearly forty-five minutes ago."

Pushing his chair back from the table, he pulled on his coat and grabbed a flashlight. "You all start eating; I'll be back soon."

His brother stood up too. "I'll go with you," he said.

"Good." Dad nodded and grabbed another flashlight.

———————————————————

Out in the pasture, Emily hadn't gotten very far. It was completely dark now, as clouds covered the night sky. Home was just beyond those hills, she knew, but the hills she enjoyed climbing during the summer now blocked any glimpse of its glowing lights.

Emily had found a thick stick to lean on, but it wasn't really long enough. Any pressure she put on her foot made her cry out in pain, and she would sink to the ground every few steps to rest before going on.

Tears ran down her cheeks as she considered the long distance that lay ahead of her. Would she ever make it to the house? Mom and Dad would be worried. Dad would come out and look for her, but how would he ever find her? It was so dark; the pasture was so hilly, and no one knew where she had gone. Swallowing back a sob, Emily pushed herself up and took another step.

She may have gone on like this all night, but a sound broke through the stillness of the night. A dog barking! Polar! How the sound warmed her heart.

"Polar!" Emily shouted. "Po-o-o-lar! Here, boy!"

Her heart pounded as she waited. Would he come? Would he leave the sheep? Emily strained her eyes to watch the hillside. And then, at last, she saw him, galloping down the long hill and up the next rise toward her, a streak of creamy white.

Anxiously, the dog pranced around the girl, licking her face and urging her to walk on with him. But she couldn't. "Go home, Polar!" Emily commanded. "Get Dad."

She gave the dog a pat and pointed in the direction of the house. "Go home!"

Polar hesitated. He ran a few steps forward, then back to Emily. He whined and whimpered.

"Go!" Emily commanded again, and he went…back to the sheepfold.

"No!" Emily cried, but the loyal dog was gone, back to his work of protecting the sheep.

Why *had* Polar barked? Emily wondered. And then she knew. The hair on the back of her neck prickled as she heard the howl. Coyotes. They were after the sheep…or anything else that was weak and injured.

An icy fear washed through her, and before she could think, Emily was scrambling over the bumpy ground, back to the tree line. Dizzy from pain, she seized a branch from the nearest tree. Terror propelled her up onto the branch, and from there to the next branch. Her breath came in gasps, and her hands shook violently as she clutched each branch.

Oh, Lord, her heart cried out again and again. *Help me! Hear me!* She couldn't say more, as her mind filled with images of hungry coyotes with snapping jaws.

The first flakes of snow were falling as Dad reached the pasture with his brother. They had called Emily's name all along the way, but there had been no answer. Now, as they followed the fence line across the hilltop, Dad called again.

It was Polar that came to meet them. The dog barked frantically, running the length of the fence and back again.

"What's the matter, boy?" Dad asked. "What's going on?"

Then Dad heard it too: coyotes.

"Are they after the sheep?" Emily's uncle asked.

Dad nodded. He looked up at the heavy cloud cover. "Looks like snow, though. The coyotes shouldn't be a problem, then. The storm will keep them from hunting."

A snowstorm, and Emily missing! Dad frowned and broke into a slow jog. Polar joined him.

"You circle the pasture that way," he told Emily's uncle, "and I'll go this way. Stick to the fence line and you'll come full circle. If we don't meet, just follow the farm road back to the house."

A single snowflake landed on Emily's face, and then another. Her nose wrinkled as she tried to brush it away without letting go of the branch. She looked up. More flakes shook loose from the clouds overhead, falling faster, thicker; it was a snowstorm.

Emily sagged against the tree trunk as relief washed through her. Coyotes didn't hunt in snowstorms, Dad had often said. From her heart rose a prayer of thanks. Those dark clouds that hid the stars were carrying snow. How the Lord was ready to hear her prayer before she even called to Him!

It was still dark. It was still cold. It was still lonely. But the icy terror was gone. Emily knew she was not alone; God was watching over her.

It was a long wait, and the cold seemed to creep through her coat and sweater into her very bones. But at last Emily saw a spot of light moving beyond the curtain of falling snow.

"Dad!" she called, and a blur of white came galloping toward her.

"Polar!" she shouted. "I'm up here!"

A moment later she was in Dad's arms, her head cradled against the rough fabric of his coat and her foot carefully supported by his arm.

It wasn't long before the cozy lights of the house shone up ahead. Her uncle met them on the porch and held the door for Dad to carry Emily inside. Instantly she was wrapped in the warmth of a steaming kitchen, her mom's embrace, and the love of family.

"Found her," was what Dad said. "Well, Polar took me to her." He carefully set Emily down on the couch and then just stood there looking at her. "Our little lost sheep has been found."

Amid all the rejoicing, Emily couldn't help thinking of the Good Shepherd who would leave the flock to search for one missing sheep.

It must be a little like this, Emily thought, as she looked at the joy on all the faces around her: *the rejoicing of the angels in heaven over one lost sinner who is found.*

JESUS, SHEPHERD

Jesus, Shepherd, show my sin—
All the darkness here within;
Make me sorry, help me pray,
And to love Thee more each day.

Jesus, Shepherd, teach the way
I must live from day to day;
Give me grace to keep Thy law
And to love, as I am taught.

Jesus, Shepherd, lead me on
To the place where Thou hast gone.
Every year I live on earth
Show me more my Shepherd's worth.

18. Ahead of the Storm

"I can see the ocean!" Wesley shouted, although his brother and cousins were right beside him in the van. "Right there! Between the trees and that big house!" He rolled down the side window to see better. Sure enough, one more city block of driving, and the great blue of the ocean stretched out to the horizon.

"That is so weird!" little Sam said. "One minute we're driving through town and the next minute we're at the end of the world!"

"It's just the ocean," his cousin Ava said in surprise. "It has to start somewhere."

Dad pulled into a parking spot next to Uncle Rob, and kids tumbled out of both vehicles. It felt good to stretch after the long drive from Uncle Rob and Aunt Shelley's house in Pennsylvania. Reluctantly, the children loaded their arms with folding chairs, coolers, towels, sand toys, and umbrellas.

"Man! There's enough stuff here for an army!" Wesley sighed, as Dad balanced a surfboard on top of the cooler he was carrying. But at last the two families were hobbling over the hot sand. Snatching their swimsuits from the bags, the kids raced each other to the changing rooms. In a flash they were back at the water's edge.

Wesley sucked in a deep breath as the cold water lapped over his feet. The waves that towered in the distance before crashing and rolling up the beach were nothing like the gentle waves of Lake Erie back home. "We are now leaving North America," he announced in a deep voice as he stood poised with his board. "Prepare for takeoff!" And with a wild yell he splashed out into the surf.

Sam was at his heels. Turning their backs to the waves, they braced themselves as a great splash of water tumbled over them, pushing them toward shore. This was fun!

"Try diving into a wave, Wes!" Ava called. "You won't even feel it hit you."

Wesley braced himself and waited. Three smaller waves rolled past. There it came—a big one. Holding his breath he dove headfirst into the wave. As Ava promised, he didn't feel the impact, but he still came up sputtering. "Ugh! That tastes awful!"

Ava waded over, laughing. "Tastes?" she commented. "What are you tasting the water for? It's saltwater, of course."

Wesley shook his head, trying to expunge the taste from his mouth. "I'm getting a drink from the cooler," he said.

Sam joined Wesley as he began wading to shore. "The water tastes funny—," he began, when a tremendous wave hit them from behind. Catching them up in its force, it tumbled them head over heels, sweeping them up the beach and dropping them there. Wesley struggled to get his feet back under him. But the wave was not through with them. Rolling mightily back down the beach, it sucked the two boys back out and dumped them in the surf.

Wesley was quicker this time in finding his footing. He stumbled over to where Sam was floundering in the knee-deep water.

"Watch out!" Ava called from behind. "Here comes another one!"

Wesley grabbed Sam, and the two braced themselves against the wave, keeping their feet firmly planted.

"I got sand in my hair!" Sam complained as they trudged toward Mom and Aunt Shelley.

"I got a huge sand burn on my back," Wes added, "from being dragged down the beach!"

Uncle Rob met them halfway to the beach chairs. "Never turn your back on the ocean," he laughed as he threw them a towel. "It'll get you every time!"

And so two vacation days slipped by, filled with learning to ride the waves, eating sandy potato chips, building a massive sandcastle and watching the tide come in to fill the moat, flying a kite on the sandy dunes, and burying one another in the sand. It was all so much fun, but Wes's favorite activity was after they had showered and eaten supper at the beach house. Then they would all go for a long walk down the shore. The sand was cool beneath their feet, unless you dug your toes in deep, Wesley discovered. Then you could find a slight warmth, a hint of the noon-day's heat. Rolling up their pant legs, the boys would race one another down the hard-packed shoreline. With no finish line in sight, they stopped only when their sides ached and their chests heaved for air. Then they looked back to see their footprints being washed away from the silky smooth sand at the water's edge.

"The weather forecast says rain and thunderstorms tomorrow," Uncle Rob said at breakfast on the third day. "Maybe we'll take you all to the aquarium in the next town. You can see some sharks up close, an alligator or two, and touch a horseshoe crab."

"Yeah! And see different kinds of turtles," Ava added. "I love them; they're my favorite."

"Are there any seahorses?" Sam asked Uncle Rob. "They are my favorite."

"You kids run out to the beach with Dad," Mom said as she began clearing the table. "Enjoy the sunshine while we have it."

After an hour of splashing in the surf, Wesley came up to dry out on his towel. He was so cold and tired from fighting the waves that stretching out on a sun-warmed towel felt wonderful. He overheard snatches of his uncle talking with his dad—"...severe storm warning with high winds..."—but paid them little attention until Mom and Aunt Shelley called from the boardwalk. "Kids! Come on in! It's time for lunch."

"Already?" Wesley wondered.

"Yes," Uncle Rob said. "We have to head out soon. There's a severe storm warning, and we have to get back home before it hits."

"Back home!" Ava and Wesley exclaimed together.

"Yes," Dad said. "There's no telling what kind of damage there will be. We have to get back to Pennsylvania to Uncle Rob and Aunt Shelley's place."

"Does that mean we can't go to the aquarium?" Sam asked.

"I'm afraid so," Dad said as he began collecting their belongings off the beach.

The children didn't know what to say, but their somber faces showed their intense disappointment.

Wesley stood on the porch amid the flurry of activity until Dad propelled him into action. It was hard to believe the hourly updates on the storm as it rolled inland and up the coast. It was a beautiful, sunny day! But before long they were all packed back in the vehicles.

They had been driving for an hour when Dad said, looking in the rearview mirror, "See how the sky is growing dark behind us?"

Wesley twisted in his seat to peer out the back window; sure enough, a heavy gray sky filled the horizon.

Sam frowned in concern. "Drive faster, Dad," he said, "so the storm doesn't catch up to us."

"We can't go any faster than all the traffic around us," Dad replied. "It looks like everyone is trying to get out of the area." The highways heading north were packed with cars, while few cars were heading south.

They pulled into a gas station when Uncle Rob needed more fuel. The wind had really picked up; lifting paper waste from the garbage cans, it swirled it wildly along the pavement before tossing it into the air.

"Hold onto your hat, Wes!" Ava shouted as the two of them dashed into the gas station to use the restrooms.

There were a few vehicles waiting for gas, so the cousins amused themselves by playing tag around the picnic tables. A boy about Sam's age was sitting on one picnic table. He joined them in their game, as did his older brother. When at last they grew tired, they all sat in a row on the picnic table.

"What's taking Dad so long?" Ava wondered.

"He's over there," Wesley pointed, "talking to some people."

"That's my mom and dad," the older boy told the cousins. "We're going to North Carolina."

"But there's a huge storm moving through!" Wesley exclaimed. "Houses are being flattened and trees ripped out by the roots!"

The boy shrugged. "Dad said it'll be fine. There are always storms along the coast. It's nothing to get worried about," he said, but he sounded worried.

"They're just plain stubborn." Dad shook his head as he climbed into the car and started the engine. "With all the storm warnings, and the rain and wind nearly upon us, they're heading right into the eye of the storm."

"Just like the painting hanging in Grandma's house," Sam piped up. "They're traveling on the broad road that leads to destruction."

"Well," Mom said, "we all are born sinners, traveling that road. Unless we repent of our sins, we'll rush right on into the storm."

It was quiet for a moment in the car, and then Sam said, "It doesn't really seem like sinners are traveling to destruction. Everything seems nice, just like the people having fun on the broad road in the painting."

"Yeah, but you can see where the road ends up," Wesley explained. "There's all fire at the end. Just like it seemed sunny down by the shore, but actually a storm was coming and we had to leave quickly."

"And we left," Dad said, "because we *believed* the storm warnings we heard. That's why God's children are called *believers*. They've believed the warnings about where their life is headed, believed in the Lord Jesus Christ, and repented of their sins."

"Yeah," Wesley continued. "And *unbelievers* just keep traveling along, ignoring the warnings…just like the family at the gas station."

"Traveling right into the storm," Sam added soberly.

You are traveling down life's road too. Which direction are you headed?

MY FEATHERED FRIEND

(Isaiah 11:6–9)

I found him lying on the deck,
My golden feathered friend.
Each day I'd watched the sky for him,
But now it was the end.

Each morn' he'd hopped up on the rail
And cocked his little head
To ask me for a crumb or two—
A bit of seed or bread.

I loved to watch his feathers blow
In autumn's blust'ry wind,
And look for footprints in the snow
From feet so strong, yet thin.

In spring I found him plucking seeds
From dandelion heads,
In summer gathering thistledown
To line his nest's soft bed.

I watched him bob across the yard
With worms for young to eat,
Then settle on a branch to call
Chic-o-ree! Chic-o-ree! Chic-o-ree!

But now he lay here, silent, still,
His body stiff and cold.
How could that feisty life be gone—
A memory to grow old?

Had God created him for this?
To live but then to die?
No, it was man who sinned and brought
An end to every life.

How sad! Yet we can joy in that
New world to come, where death
Is conquered and our sin cannot
Cut off a single breath.

19. A Break from Spring Break

"So, what are you doing over spring break?"

It was the question Clayton had been trying to avoid. The guys were shooting basketballs on the court at recess, and they all stopped to listen to his answer. Mike was sleeping over at Rick's house, Carl was going to an indoor water park with his family, and Travis and Kyle said they could stay up late every day and then sleep in till noon. Not him. Clayton would be stuck doing chores.

It wasn't that he minded helping Dad out in the barn. Most of his life he had been glad to escape the indoors and the chores Mom thought up in the house. But hearing his friends at school had opened his eyes to a whole new world—a world of leisure.

But now the guys were waiting for his answer. Clayton mumbled something about relaxing, then made a dive for the basketball. *Am I the only one whose parents think spring break is a chance to catch up on schoolwork and farm chores?* Clayton wondered. He knew what Dad would say if he complained: "A change is as good as a rest!"

Clayton sighed. Ever since he could remember, their family was living on changes instead of rest. They were always busy.

Clayton dropped his duffel bag on the end of his bed with a thump. "How many clean shirts should I bring, Mom?" he called while staring dully into an open dresser drawer. And then, "How many clean pairs of pants?" And, still without turning around, "How many socks?"

"Nine," his sister said, passing his open doorway. "Four for your left foot and five for your right."

"Nobody asked you," he said.

"Well, maybe you should stop calling Mom and figure it out yourself."

Clayton let a stack of T-shirts fall to the floor and trudged downstairs, socks in hand. It was his own fault, he supposed. He had complained so much that Dad had finally told Mom to send him to Uncle Phil and Aunt Kim's. They were in the greenhouse business, and with spring around the corner they would be busy.

He could already hear the guys at school. "So, what did you do over spring break?"

"I, uh, stayed at my aunt and uncle's."

"Cool. What'd you do there all week?"

"Uh, plant flowers."

That was totally not going to work.

Clayton entered the kitchen. "Mom!" he began again, and then stopped. She was talking on the phone. She was turned away and didn't seem to have heard him.

"Well, Kim," she was saying. "This is really nice of you. Clayton does seem to need a break. Yes, they do work them hard in school these days. A few good nights' sleep and lots of time to relax should be just the thing for him. Yes, we'll stop by the library and be sure to take some books along. Good, good, we'll see you then."

Clayton ducked back out of sight as Mom hung up the phone. *He needed a break? They worked him hard in school? It was about time Mom and Dad realized that! Now they were sounding like everyone else's parents. Not that he put an enormous amount of effort into school, but still, a kid was entitled to a break too.*

Clayton took the stairs two at a time. "Lots of time to relax" had been Mom's words. Suddenly he could figure out how many socks to pack.

"Now you get yourself a good night's rest," Aunt Kim said from his doorway. "And don't you go setting your alarm. I'll be back in from the greenhouse about eight to get you your breakfast."

And what a breakfast it was. *Every boy deserves a spring break like this,* Clayton thought while stuffing some egg into his mouth alongside the sausage. *It gives new meaning to the word "break!"*

"Oh no, don't you touch those dishes," Aunt Kim said after breakfast, and shooed him out of the kitchen.

Clayton almost felt bad leaving one person to clean up all that mess. Uncle Phil had already pulled on his coat and headed back out to the greenhouse. Back home everyone pitched in with cleaning up the dishes, and it took no time at all.

Well, Aunt Kim probably liked doing dishes. Clayton went upstairs to get his book. Then he sprawled himself on the couch and read. Uncle Phil came in later to grab a cup of coffee. Clayton was glad to be left to his book again. He was never free from interuption at home.

Lunch already? Clayton looked up in surprise. He wasn't surprised when Aunt Kim shooed him off again after lunch, though. "No, no, you run along," she said with a smile. "I've got the dishes."

Wandering back into the family room, Clayton picked up his book. His hero was in the thick of danger, but somehow he'd lost interest. Wandering to the window, he watched as a teenage boy a few years older than himself helped Uncle Phil move trees across the nursery. *Were they making room for a new shipment or setting up the nursery for opening day in a few weeks?* Clayton wondered.

A dog ambled into view and, catching sight of the dolly, charged it, barking playfully. Uncle Phil hollered at it, and the dog wandered off again, nosing the ground along a row of cedars.

Clayton brightened. He had always liked dogs. Hurrying to the mudroom, he pulled on his coat and shoes. "Hey, boy!" he called. "Come here!" He waved a stick enticingly. "Go, fetch!"

But after a few rounds of fetch the old dog was tired. Lying down with the stick between his teeth, he refused to bring it back. *You're just going to throw it again,* his eyes seemed to say. *I know you will. And then who will have to go fetch it? Forget it. I'm done.*

Clayton gave up and walked over. Reaching down, he rumpled the dog's ears. "Come on, boy. Let's go see what they're doing in the greenhouse."

Slipping in the side door, he expected to be greeted by a wave of hot, humid air, but it was surprisingly cool inside. The dog bounded ahead as it spotted Aunt Kim working at the planting belt with another woman and a younger girl.

"Shoo, Shep!" she said. "You shouldn't be in here!" Her eyes found Clayton. "Ah, you needed to stretch your legs, I see. Well, go right ahead. There's an old bike in the shed, and there might even be a skateboard you can take out back to the concrete area."

"Cool!" Clayton ran off. But there wasn't too much point to biking, he soon discovered, when there was no one to bike with or anywhere to go. Back home there was always one of his sisters to race to the barn, or his dad to go meet out in the field. He had never been great at skateboarding, but he tried it for a while, and that was more satisfying. But when he put the skateboard away and looked at his watch, it was only four-thirty.

He stood by the shed door for a moment, watching the activity in the nursery. The older boy was loading skids for Uncle Phil to move with the forklift. Clayton wondered how old he was. Uncle Phil caught him staring and waved. Clayton waved back and quickly turned to go in. Back inside he wandered around for a few moments getting a drink and looking at stuff on the bookshelves before at last picking up his book. It was so quiet.

He was relieved when Aunt Kim came in later to start supper.

Do you need any help? That's what he would have liked to ask as he watched her chopping vegetables at the table. It would have been an excuse to join her in the kitchen, but the words died on his tongue. *No, no. You run along and relax.* He could already hear her answer.

Clayton didn't have much to add to the discussion over dinner. Everyone back home was doing well. School was going fine. He'd had a relaxing day, thank you. But there were no awkward silences. His aunt and uncle chatted about their work in the greenhouse.

"That Jack, he can really work," Uncle Phil said.

"His sister works hard too," Aunt Kim added. "I'm going to miss her when she goes back to school."

"They should be able to put in some after-school hours once it gets busy, though," Uncle Phil put in. "We'll need the extra hands then, that's for sure."

After the supper dishes had been done, Uncle Phil stretched out in the easy chair. "Ah, that feels good," he said. "Nothing like a deep chair after a long day. And a cup of coffee," he added as Aunt Kim came in with two steaming mugs. Clayton could imagine how good it must feel to stretch out in that chair after a long day of work. He, however, felt restless. He wanted to *do* something.

"Now, what game shall we play?" Aunt Kim asked while setting down the tray on the coffee table. "Risk? Scrabble? Monopoly? What's your favorite?"

Clayton brightened. *This was more like it.* He had been dreading a quiet evening with his book.

<hr />

Morning dawned, and Clayton sprang out of bed. Was he too late? He had forgotten to set his alarm. Scrambling to pull on his clothes, he opened his bedroom door. He heard voices below, and then the back door banging shut. It was quiet again. Clayton slumped against the door frame. *Now what?*

Trudging back into his room, he dropped down onto the bed. He should have just slept in. Not that he knew how. The moment the sun cracked the horizon, his eyes cracked open too, it seemed. But it just hadn't been early enough.

Clayton would never have guessed how hard it was to be idle. He felt more tired and sluggish than after a long day of haying out in the fields with his dad. He toyed with the idea of starting breakfast. *Nah, I'll probably make a big mess,* he thought. He wasn't that handy with food in the kitchen. *I mean, I could make a sandwich,* he told himself, *but the stove and the frying pans are out of my league. No matter how golden things start, how merrily they sizzle, they come out black in the end.*

⇢──── ⇠⇢ ⇠

"You tearing through that pile of books you brought?" Uncle Phil asked around a mouthful of eggs.

They had just finished breakfast, but Uncle Phil was working on seconds. Clayton was still at the table trying to finish his first helpings. His appetite just wasn't there.

"Yeah,…no," he stammered in answer to his uncle. "I finished one book, but I was thinking maybe I would save the rest for later."

"Good thinking," Uncle Phil replied. "You'll want something to read this afternoon."

Clayton gulped down some orange juice. It was now or never. "I, uh, was wondering if you could use some help out in the greenhouse." He bent down and suddenly became busy loading his fork with bacon. "Thought Jack could maybe use some help moving stuff around in the nursery," he added.

Still busy with his fork, Clayton missed the grin Uncle Phil flashed at Aunt Kim. "You know, Clayton," he said leaning over the table toward him. "We've got a shipment coming in with a lot of shrubs to unload. I was hoping you'd ask!"

"You were?" Clayton's head popped up. The bacon was forgotten as he jumped to his feet. "Great!" he exclaimed and was halfway out the door before Uncle Phil could push back his chair. "I'll grab the extra dolly from the shed," he called over his shoulder. Suddenly he didn't care what the other guys would think. Let them sit around or sleep in till noon. He had better things to do.

THE MASTER'S WAY

(John 13:1–17)

Their feet were hot and dusty
From the roads they'd walked that day,
But not a single servant came
To wash the dirt away.

The friends of Jesus just sat down—
Their feet would stay that way.
"There's nothing we can do to help,"
Their silence seemed to say.

But Jesus rose and filled a bowl
With water, took a towel,
Wrapped it around his waist, and knelt
To serve in that last hour.

He lifted and then gently rinsed
The dirt and grime away,
Then dried those feet and sat back down;
He'd shown the better way.

"You are not greater than your Lord,"
He told his friends. "And you
Must also serve with joy to find
A happiness that's true."

20. Laughter in the Woods

"My hands and feet feel frozen!" Lea said from where she lay in the snow.

"Stop being such a baby," her brother, Walter, said and rolled over to fling some snow at her. They were visiting their cousins in northern New Jersey. After one last ride down the hill, they had all tumbled in a pile at the bottom. Now they were lying on their backs trying to catch snowflakes on their tongues.

"Ugh!" Lea sat up to brush the snow from her face. "You got it in my ear!" she told her brother.

Walter just laughed. "That's not your first ear problem. Remember the time we were visiting the new neighbors and you stuck your head through their porch railing?" he asked with a grin. "We couldn't get it out," he told Brad and Melinda. His smile grew wider as he began to laugh. "Her ears were too big, so we had to pull the rest of her through the railing and out the other side!" Brad, and even Melinda, joined in the laughter.

Lea just glared at Walter. *Why was he suddenly being so mean? Just to be funny?* "Won't you ever let me live that down?" she asked hopelessly. "That was *years* ago. It's not like I've stuck my head in a railing ever since." She got to her feet, and Melinda also rose.

Brad also got up and called to Walter. "C'mon. You going to help get some wood for the campfire tonight?"

"Campfire?" his sister asked. "Up in the clearing?"

"Cool!" Lea said. "Can we come?"

But Walter spoke up before Brad could answer. "Of course not. It's just for the guys. Brad and Mark and me."

Brad opened his mouth to speak, but then closed it again. He glanced uneasily at his sister. Melinda frowned at him and turned away. "Let's go in," she said to Lea, and they turned to go. "I'm sure supper is almost ready. Better watch out for the bears!" she called saucily over her shoulder.

Bears? Lea wondered. *Were there really bears in the area?* That gave her an idea...

Lea passed Walter in the hallway as they were washing up for supper. She hurried past him without speaking.

"Come on, Lea," Walter said. "I was just joking around. You've got to admit it was pretty funny. You've laughed about it yourself. Lighten up a little."

"Yeah, but it's not like you have to bring it up in front of everyone," Lea protested. "Why don't you laugh at yourself for a change?"

Walter paused as he appeared to think about it. *Could he laugh at himself?*

Supper was noisy with the clatter of forks, the chatter of children, and the laughter of grown-ups. Lea loved watching her parents visit with her aunt and uncle. How they could laugh together when they started retelling stories from their growing up years. Through the stories, she was starting to realize that Mom and Dad had once been young just like her. They'd had the same friendships and troubles, the same hopes and worries and dreams.

Aunt Linda was talking to Dad now. "I'll never forget the time you were helping Dad paint the living room. You had just finished the last wall, and everything was picture perfect, when you jumped down from the step stool and landed on the corner of the paint tray!"

She stopped as the children erupted in laughter. "I can still see you blinking with a splatter of paint hanging off your eyelashes," Aunt Linda finished. "You were trying to convince Dad that the splotches on the ceiling were the latest look in home decorating."

Lea turned with a grin to Dad. "Really, Dad? I guess Grandpa was pretty mad, wasn't he?"

Dad chuckled as he took another bite of mashed potatoes. "That wasn't the only damage I did to the living room. Another time I was in a hurry to blow out Mom's big blue candle before anyone else could, and I tipped it, pouring blue wax all over the cream carpet. I don't think that blue ever came out completely." He took a gulp of cranberry juice. "Your poor grandma," he told the children. "What she had to put up with!"

When all the plates were scraped clean and the general hubbub of wiping sticky fingers and faces was over, Uncle Jake cleared his throat and passed out the Bibles for following along. After reading a portion from Proverbs 15, he paused before giving thanks in prayer. "What did we read about?" he asked, starting with one of his younger sons.

"Mary's heart," the little boy said confidently.

Lea caught Walter's glance and smiled before she remembered she was supposed to be angry with him. *"Mary's heart"? That little guy sure hadn't been listening!*

Uncle Jake looked puzzled as he looked down at the Bible passage again. "Mary's heart…," he repeated slowly. "Aha. Very good! 'A merry heart,' verses 13 and 15. And what does a merry heart do?" he asked the older children.

"It's good like medicine," Melinda answered. "Um, if you're not feeling cheerful, someone else who is joyful can make you feel better. Their happiness is like medicine that makes you glad."

"So, laughing can make someone feel better?" Lea asked doubtfully.

"That depends on the source," Uncle Jake said. "If it's done in fun—out of true happiness and not with the intent to hurt someone—laughter can lighten a tired heart. You see, it depends on our heart. If our heart is pure, then the joy and laughter that come out of it will also be pure."

It was while they were drying dishes that Lea thought again about the paint tray incident. Dad hadn't seemed to mind when Aunt Linda brought up that old story. In fact, he had laughed right along and told about another one of his accidents. Maybe that was because he knew she was telling it just in fun. There was no malice in her words. No intent to hurt.

Crackle, crackle, snap! It was dark in the woods as heavy snow clouds covered the moon. *Rustle, rustle, snap!* It sounded as though something was moving through the trees. And then a giggle. "Shh! Help hold your end of the garbage bag! And take your hat off! They'll spot you from a mile away!"

Crackle, crackle…crash! Melinda heaved a heavy rock onto a dead tree branch. With a splintering crack it came crashing down. Lea grinned and shuffled behind the garbage bag up to the next clump of undergrowth. The girls could see the boys gathered around the campfire at the top of the hill. They had been milling around the fire until the dog became alert to the sounds in the woods. Sniffing the air and pricking his ears, Shep had ventured to the tree line, until the boys called him back. The next series of crackles raised the fur on his neck. Brad quickly snapped the leash on his dog as it let out a low warning growl. But the last splintering crash had been too much. Even the boys could now see a black form lumbering up the hill. With a lunge toward the woods, Shep began barking furiously. Brad had all he could do to hold him back.

"That's no coyote!" The girls could hear the boys' voices. "It must be a bear!" And with a swift kick, Walter knocked down the logs in the campfire as the other two tossed snow over it.

The sudden flurry of activity caused Shep to dance wildly on the end of his leash, while out in the woods, Lea buried her face in her arms, trying to muffle the laughter that kept bubbling up inside her. It seemed the dog was on her side, for he was playing his part perfectly.

"Now run!" Walter's voice rang out, and the girls sprang from their hiding places.

"Hello!" they shouted. "Where are you going?"

The boys broke their stride and turned to peer into the dark woods.

"Hello!" the girls repeated. "What happened to your fire?"

"What?" Brad exclaimed with a frown. He stared as the girls came puffing up the hill and out into the clearing. Then his frown slipped into a look of relief. "You girls!" he said with a frustrated laugh. He shook his head and tossed a snowball at them. "You just couldn't stay home, could you?" He shook his head again and laughed. "I can't believe you got us. We were running out of there like a flock of panicked geese!"

Walter's face still wore a frown. "Nah, we were about to leave anyway," he said in a tough voice. "It was getting pretty cold out."

Brad just looked at his cousin and laughed. "Yeah, right, Walt," he said. "Whatever."

Melinda hurried over to her brother's side. "We did get you pretty good, didn't we? It was Lea's idea, and Shep sure helped with all his growling. He was almost making me scared!" She looked at Lea and laughed. "Next time they have a campfire, I think they'll let us come along!"

Lea just stood there and grinned.

Fat flakes of snow were beginning to fall, and the group trudged home through the deepening snow. The girls led the way, still clutching the giant garbage bag between them. The boys could just make out the black form of the "bear" through the giant blobs of snowflakes drifting down.

Lea turned back to the boys. "Grr!" she growled threateningly, and imitated the lumbering walk of a bear.

At last a smile began to tug at Walter's lips. It was pretty funny, actually, that they had been chased home by a giant garbage bag. "I can't believe it," he said with a wry grin. "If it hadn't been for Shep, I don't think you would have pulled it off."

Lea burst into laughter. "It sure worked. I've never seen you run so fast!" She took a few more steps, then turned and said in a thoughtful voice to Melinda, "Remember the time the boys wanted to have a campfire in the woods but were scared home by a garbage bag?" Shrieking with laughter, the girls ducked as the snowballs flew.

Walter gave a mock groan. "It's going to take years to live this story down," he called to his sister.

Lea turned around with a wide grin. "You better believe it!" she agreed.

WHO AM I?

I use my "toes" to hide my nose
When hunting fish or seal.
I paddle far—just like a dog—
The cold I do not feel.
Who am I?

On grass I munch, on roots I crunch;
I gorge when hunger calls.
But slippery fish, my favorite dish,
I hunt at waterfalls.
Who am I?

I feed by night on honey sweet—
So sticky, gold, and pure.
See on my chest the rising sun
Reflected in my fur.
Who am I?

My winter sleep, so long and deep
Lasts more than half a year.
My toes point in—they help me climb
The trees when danger's near.
Who am I?

I'm gold or brown or black or white,
Designed by God's wise care,
I hunt, I sleep, I swim, I climb—
This shows that I'm a bear!

21. Someone Special

"It's *your* turn to be the lion, Alli," Kyle declared while getting up off the ground. His sister looked at the leaves and dry grass clinging to his pants and sighed. *How much longer will I have to play this?* she wondered. Mom was busy cooking supper for their own family, as well as for another family in their church whose mom was sick. Kyle had insisted on helping Mom in the kitchen, and Mom had finally called Allison to take him outside to play. Now Allison was tired of roaring and crawling through the long grass in the ditch.

"Hey!" she suddenly said, as Kyle aimed an imaginary hunting gun at her. "Why don't we play hide-and-seek?" Hide-and-seek was not her favorite way to spend a Saturday afternoon either, but it would be better than being the lion again. "You go hide, and I'll count to twenty and then find you," she told her younger brother.

"Okay!" Kyle said brightly, and Allison watched for a moment as he began his swaying half walk, half run across the lawn. "Don't look!" he shouted back, and Allison closed her eyes and began counting.

"Eighteen…nineteen…twenty!" she soon called. "Ready or not, here I come!" And she walked over to where her brother was peering from behind a bush.

"Eighteen…nineteen…twenty!" Allison called again and again as she trudged over to the bush. *Is this the fourth or the fifth time Kyle has hidden behind that same bush?* she wondered in frustration. *Just when is Mom going to be done cooking supper, anyway?* Aloud, she called, "I see you, Kyle. It's your turn to count."

Kyle got up with a disappointed sigh. "No, Alli," he said and stamped his foot. "You have to look for me first. Look behind the shed and the garage."

"Listen, Kyle," Allison said impatiently. "If you want me to look for you, you have to hide in a *different* spot. A *secret* spot. Far away from the deck where I'm counting. Okay?"

Kyle nodded, chastened. "I'm sorry, Alli," he said without meeting her eyes. "Sorry I made you mad. Can I hide one more time?"

Allison shrugged her permission and trudged back to the deck. Sometimes it was hard to remember that her brother was special—that he needed more patience than other boys his age. *Kyle isn't trying to annoy you, Allison,* she could hear Dad say when Kyle was being especially persistent in his efforts to get her attention. *He just wants your attention because he loves you.*

"Eleven…twelve…thir—" Allison counted aloud.

"Allison!" Mom was knocking on the window. "Telephone for you."

With relief, Allison darted down the deck stairs and into the house. "Hello?" she said after picking up the receiver. It was a friend from school asking about one of their homework assignments.

The phone call took longer than Allison had expected, and she was surprised that Kyle wasn't peering in the window or calling to her from the door. *I guess he's still sitting behind that bush,* she thought as she tugged her shoes back on.

"Ready or not, here I come!" she called loudly as she stepped outside and headed for the bush. The telephone call had cheered her, and she popped playfully behind the bush. "Boo!" she said loudly, but no one was there.

"Aha! So you've found another hiding spot, Kyle!" she said cheerfully. "Better watch out! I'm coming to get you!" And she headed across the lawn to the shed. No Kyle. To the garage. No Kyle. *Well! He actually hid this time!* Allison thought with surprise. *Good for him!*

Aloud she called, "Better watch out, Kyle! I'm coming to find you!" And she checked behind the tree, around the house, and in the ditch. No Kyle. *There really aren't that many hiding places, so where can he be?* Allison wondered. *Maybe he got tired of hiding and went inside while I wasn't looking,* she decided.

"Mom!" she called as she opened the back door. "Has Kyle come in?"

"No," Mom answered. "Aren't you playing with him outside?"

"Yeah," Allison replied. "We're playing hide-and-seek, and I just wondered if he had come inside to hide."

"No, he hasn't," Mom said. "Listen. I have the casserole ready, so I'm just going to drive it over to Mrs. Chetney's. I'll be back in half an hour. Dad should be home by then, too, for supper. You keep an eye on your brother, okay?"

"Okay," Allison said and stepped back outside, closing the door.

The sun had dropped low behind a bank of gray clouds, and the cold wind stung her cheeks as she called out. "Kyle! You can come out now. You won, and we're going to play another game."

Where can the boy be? Allison wondered, starting to become frustrated again. "Listen, Kyle," she shouted. "You did really good and you can come out now!"

There was no answer. With a frown Allison began checking all the same places again. Maybe he had moved from one hiding spot to another without her noticing. It was unlikely—Kyle had never been very quiet or stealthy—but what else could she do?

Turning back from checking behind the shed, Allison glanced at the cedar hedge. *Would Kyle have gone through the hedge as he had so many times when he was very small?* Crouching, she peered through the gap. The tall grass of the marsh, dry now in winter, waved before her eyes. Holding the branches from her face, she pushed her way through the hedge and stood up. The railway tracks lay beyond the marsh, and an untended pasture beyond that.

Worry made her frown, as Allison quickly crunched through the reeds and dry stalks of grass. She paused by the railway track and looked both ways. "Kyle!" she called hesitantly, feeling foolish. Then, "Kyle! Where are you?" more loudly this time. Only the silent bite of tiny snow pellets stung her ears. Hurrying now, Allison crossed the tracks and slipped through the fence that enclosed the pasture. "No Trespassing" the sign read. But Kyle couldn't read. Hurrying over the uneven ground, her eyes searched the distance. It almost looked as though the stiff grass had been pushed down in a path leading to the far end of the pasture. Allison followed the faint path, calling loudly.

And then she heard it. A dog's bark and a muffled cry. "Kyle! Is that you? I'm coming!" Allison shouted. There were more of the hiccupping sobs, and then a terrified voice cried out, "Alli! Alli!"

Dashing up a low rise in the pasture, she finally saw him—a panicked bundle of blue caught by his coat in the barbed wire of the fence. An angry guard dog was snarling ten feet away on the end of his chain.

"Alli!" the boy screamed once again as the dog lunged for the newcomer. But the chain stopped the dog short.

In a moment, Allison had torn Kyle's coat loose from the barbed wire and was hurrying the sobbing boy back through the pasture and down to the railway tracks.

"Oh, Kyle," she said as they staggered along the uneven, frozen ground. "You can't run away like that! You could have been hurt!"

The boy shifted his wide blue eyes away from her gaze. "I'm sorry, Alli," he said with a new sob. "I'm sorry. I wanted to hide in a secret spot, but the dog was there."

Then Allison stopped and bent to look into her brother's face. "No, no, Kyle. I'm not angry at you," she said. "It's my fault. I should have taken better care of you." Briefly, the boy lifted his eyes to see if her face echoed her words. "I'm just trying to tell you that you are special, Kyle. Special to me. I love you, and I don't want anything to happen to you."

"Oh, I get it," Kyle said. And a big smile of relief brightened his face. "Don't worry, Alli," he added, wrapping his arms around her waist. "You are special too."

THE HOUSE OF GOD

(Psalm 122:1)

Is there a place in church for me
Though I am young and small?
Or is God's house for older ones:
The wise, the grown, the tall?

No! Every child is welcome here;
The Lord invites them in
To learn His laws, that with His help
They may be kept from sin.

Within God's house, the smallest child
Can sing our great Lord's praise,
Can learn from stories of the past
And ask Him for His grace.

Won't you, then, come and join with those
Whose hearts are glad to go
Each Sunday to the house of God
And bow before His throne?

22. Treasures and Daydreams

"Watch this!" Myra called as she glided around the basement floor on her rollerblades.

Kelly watched as her friend took the corner and then made a quick turn to circle the basement, skating backward this time.

She made it look so easy. The soft tap of the rollerblades was the only sound as she moved smoothly across the cool cement floor.

"Can I try now?" Kelly asked.

"Sure!" Myra said. She sat down and pulled off the rollerblades. She rubbed her toes as Kelly began to fasten the straps. "They're getting too small for me," she told her friend. "Do they fit you?"

"Yup!" Kelly said happily. "They feel good."

<hr/>

Kelly was still thinking about the rollerblades when Dad came to pick her up. "Do you think I could buy a pair of rollerblades, Dad?" she asked as they drove home. "I have ten dollars saved up from babysitting."

Dad shook his head. "Ten dollars isn't going to get you a new pair of rollerblades," he said. "But maybe you can find a secondhand pair at a garage sale."

"Oh," Kelly said in disappointment. "There aren't that many garage sales in the fall, are there?"

"Not too many," Dad agreed. "Most people have yard sales in the spring and summer."

"That's okay," Kelly said. "I don't really want a secondhand pair anyway. I want *good* rollerblades, like Myra."

Dinner hour was as noisy and busy as usual, but Kelly didn't notice. Her mind was so filled with moneymaking schemes that she couldn't have even told you what she ate for dinner. The strong flavor of brussels sprouts was washed away by the sweet dream of having her own rollerblades. Babysitting was her go-to way to earn money, and over the clatter of forks Kelly could already imagine the soft whirr of smoothly spinning wheels. Dinner was nearly over when Mom broke into Kelly's daydreams to tell her the Nelsons needed a babysitter Friday night. That's when Kelly's dreams sprouted wings.

"Do you have any homework?" Mom asked her after the youngest children had been put to bed.

"Just a little," Kelly answered. "I finished my math on the bus ride to Myra's house, but I still have a little work on the *Word and Deed* magazine."

"What do you have to do?" Mom asked, picking up the mission magazine. She flipped through the pages.

"Oh, it's on the back," Kelly said. "We have to finish the last section of the 'Young at Heart' page."

Flipping to the right article, Kelly began to read. At first it was hard to concentrate, but soon her attention was drawn across the continent to a land far less privileged than hers. Dreams of rollerblades were replaced with dusty bare feet and empty hands. The children she read about

—151—

also had dreams: dreams of going to school, dreams of owning a family Bible. Kelly suddenly realized how much she had, how much of her daydreaming was filled with "getting."

"Forget about the rollerblades," she suddenly said aloud. "I don't need them to make me happy. I'm giving my ten dollars to the mission."

———

It was a few days later at school. The ringing bell signaled the end of lunch. Kelly joined the students flocking out to the playground.

"There's a class trip next week!" Vanessa exclaimed. "It's going to be so much fun."

"My sister went last year," Leigh added, "and she said they have tennis courts and tons of smooth trails for rollerblading."

"Yeah," another girl chimed in. "We get to climb the monument and then rollerblade or play baseball and stuff during lunch hour."

Kelly could feel her heart racing. The longing for rollerblades rose up inside her again, stronger than before. How she wished she had a pair of her own!

"Do you all have rollerblades?" she asked the other girls.

"I do," most replied, while Vanessa explained that she could borrow her cousin's.

"I'm using my sister's," Leigh said. "They're too small and I get blisters from them," she added ruefully. Then she shrugged and laughed. "Oh well; it's still fun!"

Reluctantly Kelly's thoughts went to her brother's rollerblades: gray, scuffed up, with one buckle torn off. She could borrow them if she had to. The wheels were rather worn from roller hockey, and they were at least two sizes too big. *But*, Kelly told herself, *they're better than nothing... I guess.*

"Hey, girls!" Myra came breezing up to the group. "Did you hear about the class trip? If we have any energy left after climbing the monument we can rollerblade!"

"We know," the girls told her. "We were just talking about who has rollerblades."

"Well, someone can buy my old rollerblades if they want," Myra said. "They're getting too small, so I bought a bigger size, on sale. My dad said I have to sell my old pair to help pay for them."

"How much are you selling them for?" Leigh asked, and Kelly listened intently for the answer.

"Twenty-five dollars," Myra answered.

Only twenty-five dollars! Kelly thought happily. *I could have the money after babysitting this Friday.* Then her eyebrows lowered. *What if Leigh wants to buy them too?* she wondered.

By now the girls had run off to the basketball court, and Kelly hurried after them. She would get Myra alone and tell her that she would have the money by Monday.

It wasn't until after school when they were walking to the buses that Kelly could talk without Leigh overhearing.

"Save the rollerblades for me, okay?" she told her friend. "I'll buy them from you next week."

Myra shrugged. "Sure, it doesn't matter to me who buys them, as long as you bring the money."

Kelly nodded her head emphatically. "I'm babysitting this Friday, so I'll have the money for you on Monday."

"That's fine," Myra said, heading off to her school bus. "Bye! See you tomorrow."

"Bye!" Kelly managed. Her face was glowing as she climbed the steps and walked the narrow aisle to her seat. *Just wait until she told Mom and Dad!*

<hr />

"That's nice," Mom replied to Kelly's grand announcement. "But what size are they?"

"A perfect fit!" Kelly exclaimed. She hopped from one foot to the other next to the ironing board.

"But what about next year?" Mom said practically as she shook the wrinkles from a skirt. "You'll have to buy another pair. Maybe you had better wait to find a pair that's a size or two bigger."

"But Mom!" Kelly wailed. "The class trip is next week! I'll never find another good pair before then." She let her backpack fall to the floor. "These blades are only twenty-five dollars, and I'll have enough money after I babysit!" *If you don't give the ten dollars to the mission anymore,* a small voice sounded in her mind. But Kelly shook the thought from her mind as Mom shook the wrinkles from a shirt.

The iron hissed in the silence that followed. Mom smoothed the iron over another white shirt and then spoke. "You can use your brother's for the class trip," she said. "I'm sure other girls are borrowing rollerblades too."

Kelly's mouth drew down in a pout. "They're so ugly," she complained, and, dragging her backpack by the strap, she walked off into the kitchen.

The *Word and Deed* magazine was lying on the counter where she had left it last night. A girl about her own age smiled up at her from the cover. Her clothes were faded and her bare feet dusty, but a smile was on her face as she stood with her family in front of their new, tin-roofed house.

Ugly? The word ran through Kelly's mind. *When had the looks of her rollerblades become even more important than being able to join the others on the class trip?* She was disgusted with herself. "That's it," she resolved. "The ten dollars goes in the mission." She opened the fridge to pour herself a drink. "I can save Friday's babysitting money, and maybe one day there will be another pair of secondhand rollerblades for sale."

"There are cookies on the counter," Mom called from the laundry room.

"Mmm, chocolate chip," Kelly said, slipping two cookies onto a plate. "Thanks!" she called to Mom.

Now if I were a character in a book, she thought as she joined her brothers on the deck, *a rich aunty would come by and drop off a new pair of rollerblades. But I think I'll be just fine without them.* She pulled the patio door shut. *What had Jesus told His disciples about storing up treasures?* She tried to recall. It was something to the effect of *lay up treasure in heaven where it will last, not here on earth where moth and rust will ruin it.*

A breeze caught a leaf and twirled it down to the deck in front of her. But Kelly didn't see it. She was daydreaming again. This time she saw a new house being built after an earthquake had struck, a row of barefooted children lining up for school, and a family gathering around a Bible in their own language.

WHAT GOD HAS GIVEN ME

When I give my money for
The church or mission's work,
I'm only giving to the Lord
What He has given me.

When I use my mouth and feet
To spread the news of Christ,
I'm only giving to the Lord
The strength He's given me.

When I spend the time I have
To help someone in need,
I'm only giving to the Lord
The time He's given me.

My money, health, my strength, my time
Are all a gift from Him
To spend in service to the Lord,
To show my love for Him.

23. Better than Sacrifice

"You watch out for that tree!" Dad said as he shrugged into his heavy winter coat.

I knew which tree he meant. We had been watching out for that tree all spring and summer and fall. It was just a small seedling when Dad had planted it in the front lawn last spring, just a little higher than my knees.

"It's your mom's favorite tree," Dad had said as he carefully tamped down the dirt around the slender trunk. "Stays green in the winter, and she's hoping the cardinals will nest in it in the spring."

The tree had been faithfully watered every week until the snow fell, and fertilized for tree growth in the spring and root growth in the fall. Now, come winter, Dad was still thinking about Mom's tree.

It had snowed this winter. Not just a few ground-covering flurries but deep, heavy snowfalls that carpeted the lawn, one on top of the other. Everything was knee-deep in snow, even the tree. It had grown nearly a foot since Dad had planted it, and only that foot of new growth sprang fresh and green above the snow.

"We'll watch out," I said now to Dad as he pulled on his boots. I was collecting hockey sticks from the garage for myself, my brother, and a few cousins. Their family had come to spend the afternoon at our house. To my cousins' delight, yesterday's freezing rain had crusted the snow with a thin layer of ice. It would be perfect for ice hockey, even in boots!

"I'm dropping off a warm meal for Mrs. Meyers," Dad said as he pulled the truck keys from his pocket. "Stay in the side yard."

"We will," I called back and let the garage door shut with a bang. Bright sunlight dazzled my eyes as it reflected brightly off the snow. Mom's tree was sparkling in its coat of ice, but I hardly noticed as I dashed around the back of the house to join the others.

It was a rip-roaring game with the slippery ice adding a whole new dimension to our skills. A guy could take off with the puck and go for a breakaway…and it truly became a breakaway, as he hadn't any brakes. More than one of us followed the puck through the goalposts and into the hedge. But it added to the hilarity of the game, and we played until we had beaten the other team twice.

"Let's run races!"

I'm not sure who first suggested it, but we all thought it was a great idea. We could probably tell you who was the fastest on dry ground, but running on ice would be a new challenge for all of us. Who knew who might win? We were eager to find out. There wasn't much of a course in the side yard for a hundred meter dash, so the boys decided to run the course from the side yard into the front yard and back again.

"We can do a figure eight!" I added. "The bird feeder will be one pole to round, and…" My eyes scanned the front yard, then rested on the slender tree branching above the snow. "The little tree can be the other," I announced.

It was on the third race that a runner lost his footing and slid into the tree. Like an icicle, the slim trunk snapped and tumbled across the ice.

My brother and I looked at each other, then ran over to the tree. Carefully he picked up the bushy green treetop and shoved it down into the snow next to its trunk. Silently I watched, then swallowed nervously. Something didn't look right. Something didn't feel right.

The fun of the footraces had ended abruptly. The others went inside to play Ping-Pong, but I grabbed a snow shovel and started clearing the rest of the driveway for Dad.

<hr/>

I was upstairs in the hallway when a truck door slammed on the driveway below. I didn't want to look out the window. I wanted to run, to hide, but irresistibly my feet drew me to the window.

Dad dropped the truck keys in his pocket and paused to look at the sidewalk, the driveway, the shovel leaning against the porch wall. He looked at the house, the lawn…and the tree. My heart skipped a beat.

He knew. Maybe it was the newly arranged branches that gave it away. Or maybe it was the footprints all over the front lawn. In any case, Dad looked oddly at the tree for a moment before leaving the sidewalk for the front lawn. Nearing the tree, he bent and peered at it. Reached out. Touched it . . . and watched it fall over.

I dropped down to the floor and groaned.

<hr/>

"Jesse!" It was a command.

I could have heard Dad's voice ringing up the staircase if I had been in the attic! I was sure everyone else in the house heard it too. The hum of adult voices in the kitchen ceased. The patter of little feet fell still. Even the warm smells of coffee and soup seemed to evaporate in the icy silence.

"Come here, please."

I came.

—————⧫⧫————————⧫⧫————————⧫⧫—————

I wandered into the library when it was all over. I couldn't face the others yet. Great-grandpa was sitting in the rocker pulled close to the fireplace. A wool blanket lay over his knees.

"Come here," he beckoned with his hand.

I came.

"Sit down." He gestured to the fireplace hearth, and I sat, the warmth of the fire seeping through my sweatshirt and across my back. He knew I was in big trouble—his strength might have been going, but his hearing was not.

"Many, many years ago," he began slowly, "there was a king." Great-grandpa's voice was thin, and his hands trembled on the armrests, but the storytelling gleam was in his eyes.

"He was a brave leader who defended his country valiantly against the enemy. One day he and his army were sent on a mission: to destroy a cowardly people, a treacherous people. Their wickedness had reached its height, and an old prophet gave the king his mission from the Lord. This nation and their livestock must be wiped out.

"Samuel was the prophet, and Saul the king. When Saul came to greet him after the battle, he did so boldly. 'We have fulfilled our task,' were his words, but the old prophet was not fooled."

Great-grandpa sat straighter in his chair as he continued, and fire was in his eyes as he finished the story.

"'Then what is this bleating and lowing that I hear?' Samuel asked.

"'Oh, that?' Saul dismissed his disobedience lightly. 'We have kept the best of the livestock as a sacrifice for the Lord.'

"Tears must have risen in the old prophet's eyes as he saw the folly of the proud, unbending king. Saul had been a giant in his nation's eyes: the finest, the best. But now his own greed would cut off his reign.

"The prophet's voice may have wavered, but the verdict did not, as he pronounced the end of Saul's reign and the Lord's judgment: 'To obey is better than sacrifice.'"

The ticking of the clock was the only sound in the library as Great-grandpa's words sank in. I could hear again my own protests of innocence to Dad. I could see myself playing the part of a helpful son, shoveling valiantly, sacrificing a few games of Ping-Pong to fool Dad. But the old prophet's words rang in my ears: "To obey is better than sacrifice."

BE HOLY

(1 Peter 1:15)

Be holy, says the Word of God,
So take much time to pray,
And don't forget to read His Word
To feed your soul each day.

Make friends with those who love the Lord;
Make time to help the weak.
Remember that in all you do
God's blessing you must seek.

Be holy, says the Word of God.
The more you think and read
Of Jesus in your time alone,
The more like Him you'll be.

When happy or when sad, still look
To Jesus—He'll give rest.
Don't think your way is right, but trust
His Word to tell what's best!

24. Camping Woes and Wonders

"There's sand in the tent," Millicent announced with disgust. "I'm not sleeping in there."

"Well, have fun sleeping in the woods then, Miss Millipede," her brother Tom said, poking his head out of his tent. "Hope the bears don't get you!"

Milly glared at him before scrambling through the tent door. The door zipped loudly shut, then suddenly zipped back open as Milly shrieked, "There are ants in here!"

Tom came over to investigate. "That's what you get for eating supper in your tent," he said, rolling his eyes. "Next time it will be bears in your tent."

"Well, it was too smoky by the campfire," Milly protested fiercely. "I hate camping. I want to go home."

"Whine, whine, whine. That's all you do," Tom said cheerfully.

"You be quiet, Tom, or I'll—"

"I'll what?" Tom asked with a grin. "Go tell Mom?"

Milly glared helplessly at him; then, spying his bird guide on the picnic table, she snatched it up and tossed it through the trees. "Go find some birds!" she said angrily,…and then froze as they both heard the splash. The book had landed in the lake.

Milly followed as Tom dashed through the stand of trees that separated their campsite from the water. There lay his bird guide, gently bobbing along the lake bottom. Quickly, he splashed knee-deep into the water and retrieved his book. It was a soggy mess. Milly watched with a white face as he tried to peel apart the wet pages. They tore off in his hand. Tom flipped open the back cover. For almost a year now, he had been faithfully recording every bird he saw, but now they both saw that the ink in his list had run, and the names had nearly disappeared.

Milly swallowed as Tom splashed back out of the lake and walked past her without a word. She stayed by the water's edge a moment longer. *Why did I throw the book in the lake?* she asked herself. *What a childish thing to do! Of course I didn't mean for it to land in the water, but why did I throw the book, anyway?* Then she remembered the sand and the ants. They were not a very big deal, really. She could simply take the dustpan and sweep them out of her tent. The real problem was that she just hated camping. Everything got so dirty. Even the washrooms were dirty, and it was a five-minute hike to the nearest showers—and cold water showers only.

Milly frowned before turning to go back to the campsite. Through the trees she could see Tom balancing the book on a rock near the campfire. *The ruined book*, Milly corrected herself and grimaced. *What will Mom and Dad say? It was Tom's birthday gift, and now I've ruined it.* Slowly she trudged back to the campsite.

Getting the dustpan from one of Mom's unending bins of camping supplies, Milly shook out her own and her sister's sleeping bags and began sweeping out the tent. Tom busied himself bringing over some more wood for the fire. And that's how Mom and Dad found them.

"Well, it's a nice place we picked," Dad said cheerfully as they came back from a walk through the campground with the three younger children. "It's pretty rugged on this end, but back by the front entrance they have a volleyball court and a roped-off swimming area. You kids should enjoy that."

He stopped and looked at his silent older children. "What's going on here?" he asked.

Tom didn't answer. If he wasn't going to accuse her, Milly would have to take the blame herself. "We were arguing, and I threw his bird guide into the lake," she admitted, glancing up quickly and then looking back down at the ground.

"Is that right, Tom?" Dad asked.

Tom nodded silently without taking his eyes from the campfire.

Milly swallowed. Tom sure was angry with her. "I'll buy you another one," she said softly before stooping to climb back into the tent she was to share with her sister. She gulped as she did so. It would cost at least thirty dollars, she knew, and she had only the twenty-five dollars she had been saving up for a whole series of horse books. *But it's your own fault,* she told herself as she spread out the sleeping bags once again. *Your own fault.*

Dad called Milly to join them for some singing around the campfire, but the singing was not very vigorous. Both Tom and Milly still wore a sober face. *Will Tom ever forgive me?* Milly wondered as she glanced quickly over at him. His expression gave nothing away. Tom was like that, she knew. He could be mad for days but never do anything about it. Not like her. When she was angry, everyone knew it—her door slammed, she complained loudly, and once she had even broken her toe from angrily kicking her dresser.

After singing, Milly slowly zipped the tent door shut. Quietly she pulled on her pajamas and crept into her sleeping bag. Silently she lay listening to the night noises and the murmurs of Mom and Dad by the fire. Now Tom was the angry one. He wouldn't be kicking anything. No, he wouldn't even complain. But the fun was over. Although she always seemed to complain about the dirt and the lumpy sleeping mat, camping was usually still bearable with Tom around. He could always think of something fun to do. He could always crack a joke and make her smile—even when she didn't want to. But now she had spoiled the trip with her nasty temper. It seemed as though she would never learn to control it!

Milly sighed and rolled over, pressing her face into her pillow. She would pray for forgiveness and ask once again for strength to control her temper. And tomorrow? Well, tomorrow she would ask Tom's forgiveness. Yes, that's what she would do. And if he would forgive her, and she were to buy him a new book to replace the one she had ruined, well, then maybe the camping trip wouldn't be spoiled. With plans to earn more money spinning through her mind, Milly fell asleep.

"Pssst, Milly!" a voice whispered outside her tent door.

Milly sat up, wide awake. It was Tom!

"Come on out to the lake," he whispered. "Quickly, but be quiet!"

"What?" Milly whispered, confused. But he was gone. That was just like Tom, always up to something, even in the middle of the night.

Pulling on a sweatshirt over her pajamas, she tugged on her shoes and crept outside. Brr! It was chilly and also a little spooky creeping through the woods without a flashlight. A branch snapped and Milly jumped. *A bear!* she thought in panic. *With a big black head, coming to get me.* Her legs turned to jelly as the bear spoke. "Coming?"

"Yes," she said weakly and followed Tom to the water's edge. It was lighter here in the open, but still she heard them before she saw them. A hauntingly beautiful cry came echoing over the water toward them.

"Loons," Tom whispered. "See them?"

It took a moment of searching, but then she saw them: three black heads gliding silently through the water.

"You can write them in your bird guide," Milly whispered. "Your new one, I mean." She looked at him. "Do you forgive me, Tom?" she asked.

"Sure," Tom said. "I shouldn't have teased you about the ants and the bears." He turned to head back to their campsite. "Especially the bears," he added with a grin. "Because there's one right behind you!"

Milly jumped, then laughed in relief. The old Tom was back.

TWO WORDS

(James 5:17)

Two words are always hard to say;
It's like a giant blocks their way!
They're not big words, not hard to spell,
Not words I can't remember well.

"I'm sorry"—only two small words,
Two words, though, not too often heard
To come from my mouth willingly
Because this giant quiets me—

This giant, Pride, it tells me how
Wrong *others* are and will not bow
To humbly say, "Well, I'm wrong, too.
Forgive, please, what I did to you!

"I shouldn't say such angry words;
Or leave you out; I should have heard
Your good advice—gave back your toy."
My "sorry" could have brought back joy.

I'll ask the Lord to help me slay
This giant, Pride, so day by day
I'll see the fault that lies within
Myself, and then confess my sin!

25. Hungry Inside

Moteli's eyes grew bigger and browner, if that were possible. The biggest, yellowest pumpkin she had ever seen was sitting on the counter, waiting to be cooked. Mm-mmm! What could be more delicious than cooked pumpkin with spiced maize meal? She could eat till she burst, and no one would say, "That's enough, Moteli; we need to save some for tomorrow." For tomorrow there would be food again! Every day more pumpkin and onions, more beans and sorghum. Moteli smiled with delight. The thought of all that food wrapped her in warmth like a blanket. But it had not always been this way. Looking out the window, she remembered her days at the orphan home. She felt her cheeks grow hot as she remembered the incident with her housemother.

⊷⊷——————⊰⊰⊷⊷———————⊰⊷

"Come here, child," the housemother had said.

Reluctantly, Moteli had shuffled forward, her feet dragging over the cool mud floor.

"We have found this beneath your sleeping mat," Mma Ramnutloa had gone on quietly.

Moteli looked from her housemother down to the chunk of bread she held in her hands, then back to Mma Ramnutloa's wide brown face. Her face was serious—not angry, but very serious, nonetheless.

Still silent, Moteli felt her eyes fill with tears. They had been good to her at the orphan home, always feeding her. So how could she explain the fear that was lurking in her chest? The iron band that pressed tightly around her ribs, tight as the gnawing memory of hunger. A fear so big that even the largest helpings of sorghum and maize meal could not satisfy it. A fear that made her steal and hoard food from these kind people. How could she explain the days after her mother died, days of pinched stomachs, days when a poor old aunt who spent her days lying on a mat would creep to the door of her one-room home and throw scraps to the girl living in her yard?

"We will care for you," the housemother had said suddenly, hearing Moteli's silent cry. "There will always be food for you here at the orphan home."

But that was before. Now Moteli shook her head as though to clear it. *Those days are over*, she told herself. With another glance at the big yellow pumpkin, she began setting out bowls on the table for supper. Crossing from the shelf of dishes to the table, she glanced through the open door. A noisy bulbul bird had landed in the moporoto tree at the edge of the yard. It sang loudly, *although its song could hardly be called music*, Moteli thought. Perhaps it was not a song but a cry of hunger. Had the bird come then to take some sausage fruit from the tree? Moteli smiled at the thought of the bird trying to lift off in flight with an enormous gourd-shaped fruit in its mouth.

Fluttering down to a thornbush, the bulbul continued its search for food in a neighboring yard. Some children were playing in the thin shade of an acacia tree, and an old woman was carefully sweeping the fenced dirt yard. The bird paid them no mind as it hopped briskly from one branch to another. Why pay any attention to a thatch-roofed hut with neatly whitewashed walls when there was hunger to satisfy? Even the children did not worry him, as long as they did not throw stones at him.

Moteli watched the bird intently, the stack of bowls still in her hands. *Had it found something?* she wondered hopefully. *But even if it ate today, there was no promise of food for tomorrow,* she thought soberly before turning slowly from the door. Mma Matsapa had begun supper, and the smell of cooking pumpkin drove the thought from her mind. There was food enough here in her new home—and tasty food with Mma Matsapa cooking.

⊶———————⊷⊶——————⊷

Mma Matsapa. Moteli could well remember the day the Mma had come to the orphan home. Rra and Mma Matsapa. Moteli had seen them before, those two, last year. She and the other children had paused in their play to watch as they pulled the truck to a stop beneath a shade tree and went to speak to the matron of the orphan home. There was really a whole row of homes in the orphan compound, each with its own housemother. And life there was pleasant, as the children had their work but also their time of play. Still, they always knew that they did not belong to anyone in particular. No matter how kind their housemother, they were always one of the orphans. By no one was Moteli called "daughter."

Moteli had watched that day as the Mma and Rra had left with one of the boys. Tebogo, he was called. A quiet boy, he was. Nothing special then, but very special now. Now he had a home, and now he was "son."

And then had come that day a year later. A day when the same Mma and Rra had come for her. Climbing into the old blue pickup truck with her one extra dress wrapped in a ball in her hand, Moteli had left the orphan home. She belonged now too. Tebogo had looked solemnly at her from across the backseat as they bounced and jounced over the uneven road. *They were rich, these people,* was Moteli's thought, for many traveled by overloaded minibuses or walked great distances in the dust and heat on foot, but they had a truck!

⊷────⊷⊷────⊷

That had been last week. And now, here she was sitting at the table with Rra and Mma Matsapa and Tebogo. There would be enough food for all of them. There would always be enough. And after the meal? Almost more than the beginning of the meal, Moteli had begun to look forward to the end of the meal, for then Rra Matsapa would take down the worn Bible and, turning its thin pages, begin to fill another pinched place inside her. Love poured from those pages, from the words rumbling from Rra Matsapa's deep voice. Moteli could almost feel them filling her, warming her, bursting her chest just as the great heaping bowlfuls of maize meal and sorghum had pushed out her previously empty tummy those first few days in the orphan home.

That first night Rra Matsapa had read of the living One, the provider—a Father to the orphans, he had said. *Truly?* Moteli wondered. *Were these words the very truth? Truer even than the stories the old grandfathers told of a land where cattle were fat and the grass was always green? Was this place where the Father lived even more real than that? And could one really speak with Him? Would He really be her Father?*

Thoughts of Him filled Moteli's mind from early dawn until she lay down on her sleeping mat for the night. Hesitantly, she had begun to speak with Him. And now, as Rra once again read from the Bible, a great longing and a great fear battled in her chest. The old fear of loss was back, but this time it was the fear of losing this new, soul-satisfying food. It was a fear that tightened around Moteli's ribs as Rra continued to read, threatening her very breath. Suddenly Moteli could hold it in no longer, and with great sobs she began to weep. Rra Matsapi set down the Bible and came to her chair. Kneeling beside her, he put both arms around her.

"Oh, I am so afraid of losing this new Love," Moteli sobbed. "It is so good of the Father to love me, Rra," she explained. "And I do not want to lose Him."

Tenderly Rra explained that the Father's love was a love that could never be lost, for it was bought with the price of His Son's blood.

Once the storm of tears had passed, Tebogo helped with clearing the table. Mma Matsapi washed the few dishes, and Moteli stepped outside to water the plants beneath the shade netting. Carefully she tilted the tin can and dribbled a few drops of water onto the withered vegetable plants. There was a constant struggle to survive in this land where life was coaxed from the dry soil by single drops of water.

Moteli stood and looked out across the brown grasslands. A few thornbushes and acacia trees dotted the endless horizon. Then she lifted her eyes to the empty blue sky. He was there. Her Father. He would provide.

TELL ME

(Romans 10:14–15)

Who made the stars so brightly shine?
Tell me; I long to know.
Who makes the geese fly in a line
And tells them where to go?

Who made the fawn and leaping deer?
Tell me, who could it be?
Who made my hands, my ears to hear,
And eyes, so I can see?

Who put me here upon this earth?
Tell me, I wonder who?
Tell me His name and of His worth
So I can serve Him too.
Tell me, tell me…

Topical Index

TOPIC

TITLE OF STORY OR POEM
(Titles in quotation marks are poems.)

Adoption   Hungry Inside, p. 169

Apologizing   "Two Words," p. 168

Caring, for others' needs   Treasures and Daydreams, p. 150

"What God Has Given Me," p. 156

Church, all are welcome   "The House of God," p. 149

Compassion   Wait for Me! p. 108

Confession, don't put it off   "Today Is the Day," p. 84

Contentment   Hand-Me-Down Dog, p. 14

"Meantime," p. 100

Surprised by Joy, p. 93

Treasures and Daydreams, p. 150

"What God Has Given Me," p. 156

Coveting   Hand-Me-Down Dog, p. 14

"Meantime," p. 100

Surprised by Joy, p. 93

Treasures and Daydreams, p. 150

"What God Has Given Me," p. 156

Critical spirit   Too Much Chatter, p. 85

Death, traveling to   "Today Is the Day," p. 84

    sin as its cause   "My Feathered Friend," p. 128

Disobedience   "Day by Day," p. 19

                                        "The Saddest Sight to See," p. 77

Elderly, seeing their worth   The Red Geranium, p. 20

Eternity, traveling to   Ahead of the Storm, p. 121

Evangelism   "Tell Me," p. 174

Faith   "Heroes of the Faith," p. 49

    saving, versus historical   The Ruins, p. 43

Family Relationships, siblings   Camping Woes and Wonders, p. 163

                                        Laughter in the Woods, p. 137

                                        Second Chances, p. 50

                                        The Swindler, p. 64

                                        Too Much Chatter, p. 85

                                        Wait for Me!, p. 108

Fellowship, lost and restored   "Day by Day," p. 19

Forgiveness   "White as Snow," p. 42

                                        Camping Woes and Wonders, p. 163

Friendship, gift from God   Behind the Backstop, p. 101

    Jesus as truest friend   "Closer than a Brother," p. 107

God, as loving Father   Hungry Inside, p. 169

    as mighty Creator   Caiman and Camelids, p. 34

                                        "Who Am I?," p. 143

                                        "Just a Little Cloud," p. 33

    as teacher   Patches's Way, p. 71

    faithful and promise-keeping   When the Rains Came, p. 27

    is in control   "Just a Little Cloud," p. 33

Happiness, through service   "The Master's Way," p. 136

Holiness   "Be Holy," p. 162

Hunger, physical and spiritual   Hungry Inside, p. 169

                                        "Tell Me," p. 174

Idleness, versus work   A Break from Spring Break, p. 129

Jesus, faithful friend   "Closer than a Brother," p. 107
   as Shepherd   Missing!, p. 113
Judging by appearances   Sweeter than Them All, p. 78
Kindness   Wait for Me!, p. 108
Laughter, as medicine, as friendly   Laughter in the Woods, p. 137
Law   "The Saddest Sight to See," p. 77
     Hand-Me-Down Dog, p. 14

Leisure, too much of it   A Break from Spring Break, p. 129
Mocking   Laughter in the Woods, p. 137
Music   "Instruments of Praise," p. 13
Obedience   "Creatures of the Deep," p. 92
     Hand-Me-Down Dog, p. 14
     "The Saddest Sight to See," p. 77

Obedience, versus sacrifice   Better than Sacrifice, p. 157
Patience   Someone Special, p. 144
Praising God   "Instruments of Praise," p. 13
Prayer, for daily grace   "Jesus, Shepherd," p. 120
   for salvation   "Jesus, Shepherd," p. 120
   God hears   A Better Ending, p. 1
     Behind the Backstop, p. 101

   laziness in   "Day by Day," p. 19
Pride   "Two Words," p. 168
Reaching out   The Red Geranium, p. 20
Rejoicing, in heaven   Missing!, p. 113
Restitution, making it right   Sweeter than Them All, p. 78
Sacrifice, versus obedience   Better than Sacrifice, p. 157
Salvation   Hungry Inside, p. 169
     Missing!, p. 113

Salvation, its urgency   "Today Is the Day," p. 84
Second chances   Second Chances, p. 50

Serving others   "The Master's Way," p. 136

                                     "To Serve His Way," p. 112

Sin, caught in it   "Day by Day," p. 19

                                     "Tangled in Sin," p. 70

Special needs   French for Rachel, p. 58

                                     "Planned with Care," p. 63

                                     Someone Special, p. 144

Standing up for the right   Behind the Backstop, p. 101

Stubborn spirit   Second Chances, p. 50

Talents or Gifts, using them   A Higher Purpose, p. 8

                                     "Instruments of Praise," p. 13

Teachable spirit   Patches's Way, p. 71

                                     "The Saddest Sight to See," p. 77

Teasing   Laughter in the Woods, p. 137

Temper, unruly   Camping Woes and Wonders, p. 163

Tempter, the   "Day by Day," p. 19

Thankfulness   "Blessings from Above," p. 57

Time, for others   "Let Them Come to Me," p. 26

                                     The Red Geranium, p. 20

    using it well   "Small Steps," p. 7

Trusting God   When the Rains Came, p. 27

Unkind spirit   The Swindler, p. 64

                                     Wait for Me!, p. 108

Willfulness   Patches's Way, p. 71

Work, as a good gift   A Break from Spring Break, p. 129

                                     "The Master's Way," p. 136